THE WAY BACK HOME

CLEARING THE ENERGY
OF OUR EMOTIONAL WOUNDING

by

Bonnie Serratore

with

Werner Disse

The Way Back Home
Clearing The Energy of Our Emotional Wounding

by Bonnie Serratore with Werner Disse

Cover design by Navyo Ericsen (navyo.com)
Book layout and formatting by Agatha Malina

First Edition, 2010

Published in the United States of America

ISBN # 978-0-578-03791-2

Disclaimer:

This book is not intended to diagnose or treat any mental, emotional or spiritual illness or affliction. All information contained herein is to be used as a road map to do one's own healing work. Anyone needing more support should seek the help of a healer or therapist. All teachings and methodologies described herein were created and developed by Bonnie Serratore through years of hands-on experiential healing and her inner knowing, without assistance, guidance or information from other teachers, guides, instructors, books, schools or studies.

"All of us carry within ourselves certain beliefs and habits that prevent us from becoming the best person possible. If you're tired of these self-imposed limitations and want greater joy and fulfillment in your life, The Way Back Home will be a marvelous discovery. Bonnie Serratore is a skillful, compassionate guide whose methods have a major virtue - they work."

— Larry Dossey, MD
Author: *Healing Words* and *The Power of Premonitions*

"This book is a masterpiece that goes straight to the heart of the matter - the path to our personal freedom runs through feeling and releasing wounds from the past so we may live in the present. "

— Rod Beckstrom
Co-author: *The Starfish and the Spider: The Unstoppable Power of Leaderless Organizations*

TESTIMONIALS

"Bonnie Serratore is a profound beacon of truth. Her wisdom and healing gifts have impacted my life like no other."

— Mick Pulver
Musician, workshop facilitator and founder of the *Breakthrough Performance Workshop*

"Bonnie Serratore remains one of the most potent healers I have worked with over the last twenty years of my own healing journey. She is a true seer and has helped me reach depths that I didn't even know existed within me. I will always be grateful for the role she has played in my unfolding as a human being and as a healer."

— Aninha Esperanza
Psychologist and founder of *Rituals for Change*

"In the early 90's pure grace touched my life. While attending a workshop, I was introduced to Bonnie and her work. Over the course of the next ten years, my own life experience led me through many struggles perpetuated by old, deep emotional wounding. Had it not been for Bonnie, her clear, supportive, loving, body/mind energy-releasing sessions, I would not have discovered the freedom of being my true self.

"Even now, I am still able to move through life with more ease and assurance, my personal relationships are more authentic and I have a continuous sense of presence and grounding from within. I read *The Way Back Home* and now I am sharing it with my clients and friends."

— Tara Stone
Bowen Therapy and Emotional Release Therapist

"The work of Bonnie Serratore is unlike any I have ever experienced. She is a master in the realm of emotional healing, shamanism, awakening support, relationship coaching, and energy clearing. The depth and accuracy of her skills and talents surpass what is possible in traditional therapy.

"She has contributed significantly to my awakening over the last 15 years and her support has enlivened in me the ability to love ever greater and laugh more. Anyone fortunate enough to work with Bonnie will experience her compassion, care, and brilliance."

— Lisa Mansfield
Educator of *Liberated Living*

"Bonnie inspires courageous openings into the unexplored dark and feared places of the heart, encouraging openness and softness where there was once no previous allowance. Her experienced guidance helps to alleviate suffering by inviting one to open to all that is within."

— Jenn Starr
Yoga teacher/intuitive healer

"We used Bonnie Serratore to facilitate the 5th retreat for our YPO Forum. Our group is made up of 10 men. As the coordinator for this retreat, I knew this would be a stretch for some and outrageous for others. I shared Bonnie's CD with the men prior to the session and you could feel the skepticism in the room the day the retreat began.

"What we witnessed over 2 ½ days was nothing less that remarkable. It was real work that exposed each of our deepest selves to each other. We grew to new levels of intimacy and gained a better appreciation for one another. None of which could have been done without Bonnie's help.

"One member called this the 'Hail Mary' of retreats. We were at the jumping off point, either growing together or apart. This took us to that next level that we all talk about, but few achieve. As we approach our next retreat next month, we're still talking about it.

"In the end, this retreat exceeded everyone's expectations. I highly recommend the use of Bonnie, if you have the guts!"

— Ken Greene
Young Presidents Organization (YPO)

ACKNOWLEDGMENTS

In gratitude and appreciation to my mother Lela Cady and my father Russell (Rosario) Serratore who both in their own way set the stage for my life long quest to be free from emotional pain and put me on my path of awakening. To my brother Nathan A. Serratore who knows first hand our struggles and who fully came on board for this work. To my sister Blythe Bechdoldt, who is more plugged in to "other beings" than I am and who sparked my quest for knowledge. To my daughter Jennifer Serratore and my son Nathan Rosario Serratore, who have suffered and ultimately, allowed me to assist them in their own healing work, and who love me unconditionally. To my ex-business partner, Mollie Summerland, who introduced me to shamanism and journey work. To Neil Cohen, who brought me awareness and helped me land more deeply in my self. To Mark Adamick and Deborah Dunn, my life long friends who stood by me always and who have been through so much of life's journey with me. To Mick and Tess Pulver for their inspiration. To Bob Tripp and Cynthia Hubbard for their constant support and encouragement. To my dear friend, Lisa Mansfield, who always returns to incorporating my methodology into her work. To Werner Disse, for causing this book to happen and ultimately making my teachings available. Many thanks to Agatha Malina for stepping in and getting this project moving. To Rod Beckstrom for his faith and trust in me. To

Martha Lawrence for her support in this project. To Pablo Diaco and Danisa Perry for their continual selfless giving of time, energy, support and love. Special thanks and appreciation to Navyo for his incredible creative abilities. And especially to all of my clients and students who have placed their faith and trust in me, which allowed me to discover more ways to assist people in alleviating suffering and to do my part to raise consciousness and help humanity awaken.

Bonnie

ACKNOWLEDGMENTS

I would like to thank Bonnie Serratore for introducing me to the work and for her loving guidance. I am grateful to Anna-Lisa Adelberg for her continual guidance and wisdom in helping me unwind and understand my pain-body, and to Anna-Lisa and Lorraine DeLear for teaching the amazing Luminous Body school. Kudos to Stuart Leaf, Rod Beckstrom and Gina Wendkos for their help with the manuscript, and for being better friends than I imagined possible. Martha Lawrence was a welcome beacon of encouragement and vision. Thanks to Blythe Bechdoldt, Meri Danquah, Suzannah Galland, Meg Hobson and Valerie Carpenter for all their help and support. And I feel enormous gratitude towards Agatha Malina for lending her great talents to the book, and for bringing love into my life and helping me open my heart.

Werner

To my two children, Jennifer and Nathan Serratore, who are the reason I chose to live.

Bonnie

To my Dad, who is looking down from heaven and wondering what the hell happened.

Werner

*... and the day came
when the risk to
remain tight in a bud
was more painful
than the risk
it took to blossom.*

Anais Nin

CONTENTS

PART I

THE JOURNEY AWAY FROM OUR SELF

PART II

THE JOURNEY BACK TO OUR SELF

SECTION A

Triggers – How We Access the Energy of Our Emotional Wounding

Section B

The Dynamics of Core Emotional Clearing

Section C

Doing Core Emotional Clearing

FOREWORD

Incredible as it may seem, by our early years we have lost ourselves. Due to woundings that occur to virtually everyone before the age of seven, we let our essence—the true beauty of who we really are—slip away. Clever defense mechanisms enable us to cope and avoid the full effect of such woundings; we bury the emotional pain associated with them deep in our subconscious. As authors Bonnie Serratore and Werner Disse point out, this phenomenon is universal: "The journey away from self is part of the human experience. There is no way for us to avoid it."

As we move out of childhood, through these coping mechanisms we construct a false identity that keeps us safe from having to deal with the hurt of what the authors call our Core Wounding. As I observe the people who come into my life I witness many such façades: the Overachiever, the Perfectionist, the Controller, the Critic, the Rescuer, and the Hermit. You can name your own, because there is no limit to the number of such identities we may create. For forty years I was hiding behind the Perfectionist, always needing to be right, intolerant of mistakes, shunning vulnerability, and trying to project an image of having it all handled. Of course, the only person I was fooling was myself. Nonetheless, this false identity did a masterful job of keeping me from the intense discomfort of dealing with my core wounding.

The problem is that these false identities block us from being who we truly are and in so doing keep us separate from our very own special and unique being. And when we are so disconnected, we struggle in relationships. We are challenged to love others, yet alone ourselves. We feel burdened rather than free and we find little joy in life.

Fortunately, Bonnie and Werner offer us a powerful process for reacquainting ourselves with ourselves. It is called Core Emotional Clearing, an approach that enables us to "unwind" the energy of our emotional wounding, which in turn dissolves our false identities.

Unlike many books which offer thoughtful diagnostics but no prescription, the authors provide us with a way out of these unsettling circumstances. By following their seven-step Core Emotional Clearing process, we are able to journey back to find and claim our true selves, who we abandoned years earlier.

You'll find the book both practical and engaging. Rather then simply providing a list of seven do-it-yourself steps and sending us on our way, the book is filled with real-life case studies that show how the process has worked for others and how it might work for us.

A caveat that is made clear by the authors at the end of the book is worth noting at the beginning right here and now: There is no magic contained herein, no silver bullet. Reading the book and doing nothing will not gain you much. But if you decide to take on the work of unwinding the energy of your emotional wounding in earnest, be forewarned that it will be difficult—it will require you to experience feelings you have been avoiding for years. It will require openness and awareness on your part. It will also require persistence and in some cases tenacity from you. No doubt you will be challenged.

And when you rise to the challenge, your life can be transformed in the most magnificent of ways. While each individual will attain a result that is unique to him or her, it is not unlikely that you will experience some or all of the following: greater peace, presence, clarity, and love; positive relationships, increased assertiveness, and the freedom to live your life fully expressed.

Let your journey to self begin.

— Richard Whiteley
Author of *The Corporate Shaman* and *Love the Work You're With*

PREFACE

This book is about using energy work to improve our lives and our relationships. Let me guess what you're thinking. *Energy work. Airy fairy flaky. Hey, let's break out the crystals. Cool aura, dude. Didn't we get rid of all the witches a few hundred years ago?*

That's what I used to think. I come from a hyperrational background. I have a law degree from Oxford, where I was a Rhodes Scholar. I have an MBA from Stanford. I used to live in my brain. I used to prize intellect. I can dissect any argument or philosophy and see straight through the slightest illogic. Energy work? Give me a break.

I met Bonnie at the beginning of 2005. I was working as a lawyer and had never enjoyed it. My marriage had just ended. I felt drained, listless and under siege. A friend of mine who had done work with Bonnie suggested I see her. When he mentioned that Bonnie was an energy healer, I skeptically asked what that meant exactly. He suggested I set aside my preconceptions, including any he could plant in my head, and just visit her. See for myself. What wise words!

Bonnie rocked my boat.

My boat needed rocking. Before meeting Bonnie I baffled myself. Some people had told me I was an enviable package: intelligent, highly educated, good looking, sophisticated, athletic and well traveled. I had many of what are traditionally considered the "advantages of life," yet I felt empty inside. With the exception of my belief that I was extremely intelligent, I was riddled with self-doubt. No accomplishment, prestige job or beautiful partner changed my self-image. I was shy and had difficulty reaching out to people; forming deep bonds in romantic relationships proved elusive; I was squeamish about being assertive; I avoided taking charge of cases at work and felt much more comfortable in a supportive second-string capacity. Basically, my real expertise was hiding.

When I confided my self-doubt to somebody I usually would be met with scoffing disbelief. That was impossible—look at all I had going for me. I felt misunderstood, but I didn't hold that against anybody since I didn't understand myself either.

I tried psychotherapy. I learned a few interesting things about myself. The result, however, was mainly frustration. None of my newfound "knowledge" seemed to trickle down below the neck into my feeling better or feeling better about myself. The edge may have been taken off, but I still felt basically the same. I sensed many missing pieces. My kingdom for missing pieces.

Bonnie supplied the missing pieces. Every time I do emotional clearing work I have a significant internal shift of the below-the-neck variety. Even the first shifts, though small on an absolute scale, profoundly changed my life. Just starting the work can have a powerful impact.

My life has become easier. A lot of fear has disappeared. I feel more comfortable in my own skin. I gave up my career as a lawyer. I don't worry about money anymore. I don't worry about the future anymore. I am much more at ease reaching out to people and revealing myself. I am much more gregarious. What used to be my biggest nightmare, being at a party where I didn't know anybody, I now look at as an opportunity to meet interesting people. It feels normal to leave my imprint on situations. I have been in business situations where it felt natural to direct the process. I am more generous. I have more compassion. I feel lighter.

I jettisoned law to follow my passion for writing and have never been happier.

My life also makes more sense to me. I used to blame myself, and feel cursed, for always choosing the wrong women. Now I understand why I attracted each woman, and how each woman presented me with opportunities to heal my old emotional wounds. I no longer blame others for my misfortunes. I realize I am the creator of the situations in my life and accept the accountability (and incredible opportunity!) that goes with that realization. Bonnie's teachings have changed the way I look at myself and the world.

I also have come to appreciate that despite my initial skepticism, energy is not as "alternative" as I had believed. For example, perhaps the most famous formula in physics, Einstein's theory of relativity, is described in terms of energy. Quantum physics studies subatomic particles as discrete energy packets. On a more personal scale, the primary medical treatment of over a billion people on this planet is acupuncture, whose central tenet is that the energies within our body determine our physical and emotional health.

When Bonnie said she wanted to write a book, but was not a writer, I quickly volunteered. After all the benefits I've received, I want to help get the information out there. Writing this book has been a labor of love. It contains what I wish they'd taught me in school. What the world really needs isn't grad school, it's happiness school.

My biggest commendation of Bonnie is that I have always sensed truth in her words and actions. So have the other people with whom Bonnie has worked. I have met many of them during the course of conducting research for this book. They invariably speak lovingly about Bonnie and how her teachings have benefited their lives. Good luck to you and may you make your own good luck.

Werner Disse
Santa Cruz, California

INTRODUCTION

I am an Energy Seer. Just like doctors and lawyers, energy seers usually have a specialty. For example, some seers can see the energy of physical disease, such as cancer, tumors, emphysema or infections, while others can see the energy of missing persons. My specialty is seeing emotional energy in the physical body. I can see, sense, hear, feel and know the various layers of emotion that need attention, and can guide people to navigate these layers in order to permanently clear their emotional wounding. My expertise is healing the emotional body at the core where any trauma or shock originated.

It was because of my own healing process that emotional energy in particular enthralled me. My initial trauma and disconnection from myself began in the womb when I experienced an attempted abortion. My young mother, who was being influenced by her mother-in-law, ingested quinine, which left me with physical abnormalities. My perceived trauma continued after birth with the arrival of my sister with whom I felt jealousy, then the abandonment of my father when I was four and the continual absence of my mother due to her work schedule and social life. We were raised by our grandmother who favored our sister and tortured my brother and me emotionally and physically. My molestation began at age four and a half by my step-grandfather and two uncles. I had various health related experiences that felt traumatizing. By the time I was twelve I had become suicidal.

In my thirties, I was so miserable that I knew I had to take steps to change my life or I was truly going to end it. I had no idea of consciousness and that we create our reality, I was a victim. It was then that I began my journey back to myself. I was on a quest to be free. Over time, I found that by completely letting go, losing all sense of my self and feeling the depths of my emotions that I could clear myself of emotional pain and feel changed from within. It was my own journey that showed me how to help others.

I have been a professional healer since 1984. After several years of giving readings, teaching psychic classes and doing healing work, I began my own practice as a psychic hypnotherapist. Though I lived in a small town, I soon had more clients then I had time for. This was my own hands-on internship for understanding emotional energy in all its various forms, which helped me see into the depths of people's unconscious. I also found that I received guidance in the form of a "knowing" while I worked.

Eventually I founded a center whose focus was Core Emotional Clearing—healing the emotional body by clearing the energy of core emotional wounding—which is what this book is about. I offered spiritual and higher consciousness classes. My main activity, however, was intensive Core Emotional Clearing workshops where over the years I performed hands-on healing work on well over a thousand people, many of whom were regulars at the center. For thirteen years the center was my entire focus and love. I also trained other healers, workshop leaders and therapists, who integrated my work into their own practices.

What I've done in this book is select from my twenty-four years of hands-on experience the information that we all can use to heal our emotional wounding. No special abilities or gifts regarding emotional energy are required. With the possible exception of people who have suffered extreme trauma, anyone who has the desire to live in joy and is willing to face his or her self can do Core Emotional Clearing.

What distinguishes this book is that it describes psychology, emotional pain and healing in physical terms—in terms of energy. Emotions are a type of energy. Like molecules of air, this energy may not be tangible, but it is physical. When we suppress our emotions, this energy remains in our body and acts as a barrier that separates us from the yellow-white light of love in the core of our being that is our essence. When we are "disconnected," we are physically disconnected from our love and joy within.

The energy of our unfelt emotions also becomes part of our unconscious, negatively running our life and influencing our perceptions until we release it. When the energy of our wounds and traumas still lives inside us, we act as though the past is still happening, causing us to lead a life lacking in joy and filled with self-constraint. This emotional energy causes us to behave in ways we do not understand at a conscious level, and is the answer to many of the questions we have such trouble answering:

♥ *Why can't we just look forward and leave the past behind us?*

♥ *Why do we sometimes have such strong reactions to small situations?*

♥ *Why do we keep choosing inappropriate partners?*

♥ *Why do we often make our partner the enemy rather than being on the same side?*

♥ *Why do we keep making the same mistakes over and over again?*

There's a reason people keep searching for ways to end their suffering. Most therapies and self-help books are a band-aid; they provide awareness, but stop there. Awareness is merely the first step. I continually have new clients tell me that they have done extensive emotional work, while at the same time I see extensive dark emotional energy in their bodies.

While they had been active in their healing journey, they were spinning in circles because they did not know how to do emotional work. Awareness alone does not clear the energy of our emotional wounding. We can't just go to a doctor to physically remove it, like a cancer or a tumor. We can't think it away. We can't talk it away. We can't ignore it away.

Some people try to heal by being in the presence of gurus and teachers. While gurus and teachers can be a tremendous source of knowledge, most can provide only guidance. We have to do our own work. There's no magic wand or pill. Sorry. But that's the truth. While we may receive guidance and support, emotional healing is a solo, internal journey. In order to do it, we need to face ourselves.

This book does provide information that increases awareness. Most importantly, however, it also provides a step-by-step description of how to physically clear the pain of our past in order to live freely and joyfully in the present. We often hear that we should live in love rather than fear. This book describes how to actually do that.

We can only clear emotional energy by feeling. If we don't feel it, we won't heal it. To get through it, we have to go through it. When we fully feel the energy of our emotional wounding, the energy actually moves, changing shape, color, density and texture. Each change in color indicates we are feeling a different emotion. The energy may go from dense and dark, through a spectrum of colors, becoming looser and lighter, and eventually dissipates. We are permanently changed. We are able to connect more to the light of our love that resides within us: we are more "enlightened."

It never ceases to amaze me that when it comes to our finances, we get that it is up to us and we do whatever it takes to be successful. Yet when it comes to our emotional body, which is the true key to our well-being, many of us want a magic wand. We want our emotional healing to be both instant and done for us, without effort or accountability.

It doesn't work that way. We're dealing with the dark dense energy of our wounding that we have been accumulating throughout our life. It takes time, effort and willingness to transmute this energy.

The real question is not whether we want to feel our emotional pain, but whether we want to feel the love and joy underneath. Feeling our love and joy is the real purpose of Core Emotional Clearing. Emotional pain can be compared to a toothache. We can ignore it—and be in a constant state of discomfort. Or we can remove the tooth—and temporarily experience greater pain, but then it's over.

A huge fringe benefit of Core Emotional Clearing is that it improves not only our relationship with ourselves, but also our relationships with others. We are able to avoid the destructive patterns that commonly occur when we don't understand the dynamics of emotional energy and misinterpret our reactions. We see ourselves and our partner more clearly. We are able to be on the same side, rather than on opposite sides. Core Emotional Clearing helps create a more intimate, supportive and loving relationship: a true partnership.

This book came into being directly as a result of Werner Disse. I intended to write some form of this information back in the 1990s, but discovered very quickly that while I could lecture effortlessly for hours, writing wasn't going to happen.

When I first met Werner, he was so shut down that at the end of his first Core Emotional Clearing session I actually wondered whether we should continue working together. But he continued to do the work and quickly showed significant results. When he asked me if I wanted to write this book together I was thrilled. His unwavering commitment to his own evolution and inner freedom led to an impressive personal transformation. As a result, over time he was able to grow into the experience of the work and present my teachings in a clear and simple way that is accessible to anybody. I am eternally grateful to Werner for bringing this book to fruition.

Bonnie Serratore
Sonoma, California

PART I

*THE JOURNEY AWAY
FROM OUR SELF*

CHAPTER 1

THE ANATOMY OF EMOTIONAL WOUNDING AND HEALING

Emotions are made of energy

Though emotions are intangible, they are not abstract or metaphysical. Rather, they consist of energy that has a physical form, texture, density and color. For example, when we feel anger the energy is generally some shade of red. The density, shape and shade of the red will vary according to the degree of our anger. The energy of fear has different shades of yellow. Hate is a dark, black energy. Love for something has different shades of green or pink. Pure love is white light. Because the energy of our emotions has shape and mass, our emotions have a very real impact on our body.

We unwind an emotion's energy by feeling the emotion

Imagine a vibrant ball of energy that is moving through space with great velocity and ferocity. When it is moving freely, it will eventually burn itself out and dissipate. The same is true with our emotions.

Emotions start off as energy in motion. As an emotion is ignited, imagine that same ball of energy moving through our physical body with intensity and speed. It is our feeling an emotion that enables the emotion's energy to move. As we keep feeling, the energy continues to move and unwinds, eventually exhausting itself and dissipating.

An illustration is the grieving tradition of certain Middle Eastern countries when someone dies. The mourners, both male and female, wail and cry for days with great intensity and no constraint. They surrender to their grief, which allows the energy of their sadness to move through their bodies. By the end of this process, the energy of the mourners' grief has substantially, or completely, dissipated. Though the process may have been quite painful, afterwards their sadness and grief is greatly decreased or may even be gone. These mourners are able to keep their hearts open and continue with their lives.

Another illustration can be found in nature. A herd of impala may be grazing in peace when suddenly lions appear. The lions represent a real and immediate danger. As a result, the impala feel fear, which causes a traumatic burst of energy that helps them flee. Finally, the lions take one from the herd and stop their pursuit. The energy has passed through the impala's bodies and they shake off any residue. The fear is now gone from their bodies and the traumatic event is completely over for them. The impala immediately return to grazing, playing, walking, mating and other normal behaviors.

Emotional wounding occurs when we suppress an emotion and the energy remains in our body

When we suppress an emotion, it ceases to be moving energy. Rather than unwinding, the energy remains where it is—in our body. Over time this energy stagnates, becoming darker and denser. I will sometimes refer to this process as "emotional wounding."

Emotional healing occurs when we feel our unfelt emotions

We heal by reversing the wounding process. Just as emotional wounding occurs when we suppress an emotion, thereby lodging the energy in our body, emotional healing occurs when we feel a suppressed emotion, thereby activating and unwinding its energy.

The energy of our wounding impacts all our behavior

As we shall explore in detail later, the energy of our emotional wounding unconsciously impacts our behavior. Because this energy is still with us, we react to life as though the past is still happening. Until we clear this unfelt emotional energy, it forms part of our unconscious and influences every aspect of our life. This is why our reactions and fears can baffle us. We will not find an explanation at a conscious level.

The energy of our wounding attracts people and situations that provide opportunities to heal

As we shall see later, the energy of these emotions acts as a magnet that attracts people and situations that provide us with opportunities to feel what we didn't feel before. We can recognize these people and situations as the healing opportunities they are, or we can ignore them.

The name for this healing work is Core Emotional Clearing

Core Emotional Clearing is the name for the work described in this book. The "Emotional Clearing" part of the name comes from the process of feeling and clearing the emotional energy of our wounding. The reason for including "Core" in the name will become clearer later. In brief, this work deals with our root or original wounding—our core wounding—which usually involves feeling unloved, unwanted, separate and not enough. Core wounding is a result of our misinterpretations of events that occurred early in our life when we were immature. The work does not focus on current situations, which, as we shall see later, are still important because they serve as gateways to access the energy of our wounding.

Through Core Emotional Clearing we learn to navigate our unconscious, free from the constraints of our mind. This is the only way to effect permanent change. Our conscious mind will not get us there because thought alone cannot move emotional energy.

The benefits of Core Emotional Clearing

Core Emotional Clearing can have a highly positive effect on our life. The advantages are discussed throughout this book and include:

♥ *We become free of the traumas of the past, and stop reliving the past in the present.*

♥ *We are more comfortable in our body.*

♥ *We are more connected to our love within.*

♥ *We cease to view ourselves as victims.*

♥ *We stop blaming others.*

♥ *We liberate ourselves from the constraint of our false negative beliefs.*

♥ *We stop believing we need to be somebody other than who we are.*

♥ *We are gregarious because of our love, not because we seek the approval of others.*

♥ *We are more connected to others.*

♥ *We attract healthier partners.*

♥ *We live with less fear.*

♥ *We feel more love and joy.*

♥ *We are more at peace regardless of what is taking place around us.*

♥ *We are more attuned to our inner guidance.*

Our emotional healing is up to us

Life does not just "happen to us." We have choice. To properly understand and exercise our choices, however, we must first develop an understanding of the dynamics of emotional energy and how this energy affects our behavior. The good news is that although when we were young certain painful emotions were overwhelming, we now are more mature and have the ability to feel them.

CHAPTER 2

OUR REAL SELF – WHO WE ARE IN THE ABSENCE OF EMOTIONAL WOUNDING

As we unwind the energy of our emotional wounding, we reconnect more and more with our real self. In the absence of emotional wounding, we are completely authentic. It is important to keep in mind that because each person is unique, the real self will vary from person to person. Here are some of the characteristics that we all have in common:

We are connected to our ever present love within

At the core of our being is a brightly shining yellow-white light, which is love. Love is who we are. It can never be taken from us or otherwise disappear. It is our life force and our connection to the Divine.

We have unconditional love for our self and others. We feel joy and are at peace, no matter what happens externally.

Our desire to unite

As love already exists within us, we do not need somebody else to love us in order to feel love. This, however, does not mean we are meant to be alone. Though we can be alone, and there is nothing wrong with being alone, we have a propensity to connect and unite with one another. This instinctive desire to unite is part of our oneness and unity with all of life. It is a reflection of our desire to freely share our love and joy. We don't feel separate from others.

We feel all of our emotions, including our pain

While we always feel love, as part of our human experience we will sometimes feel emotional pain, such as when we lose a loved one. When we feel pain, our heart remains open and we don't stop feeling love. Eventually, the energy of the pain unwinds and we are back to living in joy.

We are free

We accept and embrace every aspect of our self. As we do not need approval from others, we don't hide or barter inauthentic behavior for approval. We naturally express our unique self free from fear and inhibition, enjoying life and unleashing our passions. We do not need to feel special or superior, or cause harm. We view the world as a friendly place.

We are free of our mind-generated thoughts that spin stories or produce fear. Our thoughts are just that—thoughts. They are a mirage. Whatever we are imagining is not actually happening.

We live in the present

Our mind does not distract us from what is happening in the present. This enables us to live in the present. We experience life directly, rather than through our mind. Our aliveness is in the moment, free from the static arising out of thoughts about the past and the future. We are completely in the now and therefore totally present with our feelings, our physical sensations and our day-to-day activities. Life only happens right now: the past is over and the future hasn't happened yet. By living in the present, we are able to experience life fully.

We are guided by our inner knowing

We all have an inner knowing that is independent of our mind and provides us with guidance on matters large and small. To use a trivial example, we might be at the supermarket and have a sense or knowing, which arises from within, that we need bread even though we have bread at home. When we get home we notice that the bread in the cupboard has mold. On the other end of the spectrum, we may be walking at night and somebody is approaching us. We get a feeling of discomfort in the depths of our being, and cross the street. The next day we read in the paper that the stranger mugged a couple at knife point.

Our inner knowing provides us with guidance, but has no control over our decision-making. In order to benefit from the wisdom of our inner knowing, we must have an awareness of it and act upon it.

CHAPTER 3

MOST OF OUR EMOTIONAL WOUNDING IS THE RESULT OF TAKING THINGS PERSONALLY

When we are young we tend to personalize events

As infants and young children, we often misinterpret an event to mean something about us—frequently something negative. We personalize incidents as early as in the womb and in infancy. At that age we are the center of our universe because all we can perceive are our own physical and emotional needs. Everything we hear, feel, sense, taste, touch, see and know is in direct relationship to our self. We believe we are the cause, creator and reason for everything in existence in our sphere of consciousness. We filter everything through this lens.

The effect of personalizing can be an increase of pain that leads to emotional wounding

Our personalization of events can cause our emotional pain to spike to high levels. When this happens, and we suppress the pain, we create emotional wounding. Because we all personalize situations, emotional wounding is inevitable. It is part of the human condition.

Example

Let's say we are four years old and are coloring in our coloring book with mom in the living room. After a while mom says she needs to take the laundry out of the dryer and leaves us alone. One response we might have is to feel content and continue coloring, knowing that mom will return shortly. Another possible response is that we feel alone and want mom to be present with us. This feeling may be slightly uncomfortable, but not traumatic.

Another possibility is that when mom leaves we feel alone, sad, want her to stay <u>and</u> we personalize the situation by believing mom left us because she doesn't love us. Now the level of our emotional pain likely will spike and might even become traumatic. It was not our mother's absence, however, that caused our horrible feeling. It was our false unconscious conclusion that her leaving meant something negative about us—that our creator did not love us. The pain of feeling unloved is so overwhelming that we push it down. We are suppressing our feelings. The energy of our fear and pain stops moving and remains in our body.

Our attitude towards our parents compounds our tendency to personalize situations

Our tendency as youths to personalize events is magnified by our experience of our parents as gods. They are the ones who created us, love us, feed us, nurture us and take care of our needs. As young children our very survival is completely dependent on our parents, especially our mother. This reinforces our tendency to personalize incidents: if our parents are gods, then any fault must lie with us. Also, given our total dependence on them, we might unconsciously view it as dangerous to displease or disagree with them.

The effect of parents on our emotional wounding

Most of our early wounding tends to come from interaction with our parents, both because we view them as gods and also because they tend to form most of our human contact when we are young. Emotional wounding will occur even in the most loving, kind, gentle and conscious of families because our youthful misinterpretations are the cause of most of our emotional wounding. Even when our parents' actions and words are well intentioned and non-hurtful, they are still subject to our misinterpretation. Also, since no parent can be present at every moment to cater to our every whim, need, want or desire, in our perception as infants our parents are going to fail us in some way.

Nevertheless, it is also true that our parents generally will contribute to our emotional wounding because their behavior is influenced by their own emotional wounding. So, despite their best intentions, our parents sometimes reinforce our misperception that there is something wrong with us.

Furthermore, when our parents disregard their own emotions, they are less capable of honoring ours. They then are prone to neglect our emotional life and discount our individual feelings. Many of us will personalize this neglect to mean that our emotions are unimportant or, even more damagingly, conclude that we can't trust our feelings.

CHAPTER 4

EXAMPLES
OF EMOTIONAL WOUNDING

The following are some examples of emotional wounding. It is important to keep in mind we all have unique personalities, so every individual will personalize and interpret events differently. The exact same event happening to two people growing up in the same household, even identical twins, can cause completely different emotional wounding, or wounding in one but not the other.

Infancy

As infants, absent a traumatic event we have minimal emotional wounding. We are still able to feel very keenly the energy of the emotions around us. For example, our father may be tired and irritable after work and take it out on us by yelling or handling us roughly. Or maybe our mother does not come right away when we are crying because she is busy cooking dinner, or maybe she's a single mom trying to do the work of two parents. Each parent will carry pain and anxiety into the room.

As babies we are going to sense our parent's pain and conclude that we are the cause of the pain. We might further conclude that since we caused our parents' pain there is something wrong with us. In addition, when a parent is in a bad mood and cannot feel his or her loving heart, we have a tendency to conclude that parent does not love us. These erroneous unconscious conclusions will generate highly painful emotions. If we suppress them, we create emotional wounding.

When we are hungry as infants all we know is the discomfort in our belly. We are not thinking that mom will come feed us and the discomfort will go away. We just know we are uncomfortable and we don't like it. If it frequently takes too long before we are fed, we will take it personally and unconsciously come to the painful conclusion that we must be unimportant. When we suppress this pain, or don't even know it is there, we bury its energy.

If we have diaper rash and are repeatedly left with a dirty diaper, we might unconsciously conclude our comfort and needs are unimportant. We might also become distressed because we believe we are the cause of this lack of caring, causing further emotional wounding.

If our mother is away from home on a regular basis, we long for her. We want our mother. Even if we have other loving caretakers, we will feel abandonment and separation. If our mother continues to be away, we will personalize her absence and may conclude our mother must not love us if she doesn't want to be with us. If our own mother doesn't love us, we must not be enough. Therefore, we are unlovable. When we are unable to feel this pain, the energy gets pushed into our unconscious.

As infants we tend to lack the capacity to understand what it is we are actually feeling, therefore, we feel the surface emotions, such as sadness, frustration or anger, instead of the deeper underlying emotions such as despair that we feel unloved. Because we are unable to feel these deeper emotions, we are prone to emotional wounding.

Childhood

As we leave infancy, there are still innumerable ways that emotional wounding can occur because we still tend to view our parents as gods and ourselves as being at the center of the world.

For example, when we are two years old we generally have full mobility and our inquisitiveness is in overdrive. A whole new world is available to us. We are completely open to discovering life. As a result, we seek to explore by seeing, tasting and touching our new world. This often drives our parents crazy, especially when they are tired or harassed. When we move to touch something we might get spanked, yelled at or have our hands smacked.

This is usually painful emotionally because our parents are angry with us, which hurts our feelings. We react by crying or getting angry, not realizing that underneath these emotions is a deeper feeling that our curiosity and desires are bad and therefore we are bad. We still are not emotionally mature enough to feel these deeply painful emotions. Instead, we suppress these feelings, which causes their energy to remain in our body.

If we are the eldest child and are doted on, when another sibling is born we are no longer the focus of attention. Our parents may yell at us when we try to get more attention. As two-foot-tall youngsters who take everything personally, we may misinterpret this to mean that our parents' love has been taken away and we are no longer loved. Somebody else is more lovable and has replaced us. There must be something wrong with us for this to have happened. Such a conclusion can cause a pain so overwhelming that we try to shut down our emotions in order to spare ourselves from feeling the pain.

If our parents divorce, we internalize unconsciously that it must be our fault that they are no longer together. As most of us in our heart wish for a stable home with both parents, bearing the burden of this "fault" can lead to the false conclusion that we are not enough, or even bad. Similarly, when dad sees us less, or even stops coming to see us, we can misinterpret this as further evidence that we are not lovable. We will try to suppress this hurt, trapping its energy inside us.

Traumatic events

Though there is a natural cumulative wounding process, trauma can accelerate our emotional wounding. As seen in the following examples, traumatic events act as great shocks both to our energy and our self-perception. Without a mature approach towards handling our pain, trauma can lead to our storing significant amounts of unprocessed emotional energy in our body.

Adoption

If we have been adopted, whether we consciously realize it or not, we usually have a deep-seated sense of abandonment. We have been separated from our mother in whom we lived for nine months, creating the most intimate of bonds. Though we may not have a conscious memory of the separation, it is still deeply imprinted in our unconscious. For example, Joe believed he had no emotional wounding surrounding his adoption because he deeply loved his adoptive parents. During hypnotherapy, however, when he regressed to the experience of his birth—where he was taken from his mother—the pain of the separation surfaced and he broke down sobbing uncontrollably.

When we are adopted, in all likelihood our birth parents gave us away for reasons related to themselves, such as youth, poverty, rape, illness or the inability to cope with an infant. Yet, unconsciously we often falsely interpret the adoption as meaning that because even our creators did not want us, we must not be important or worthy of love. We create emotional wounding as we take personally our birth parents' abandoning us.

Molestation

An example that universally causes profound emotional wounding is molestation. Petie, a five year-old girl, had lost her father and was very close to her grandfather. She really loved and trusted him, and they spent a lot of time playing together.

One day her grandfather took her on a car ride and asked her to fondle his penis. Petie obeyed, feeling uncomfortable, yet fearing that she would lose grandpa's love if she didn't do what he asked. At the same time, Petie experienced intense feelings of shame, betrayal and disgust. As grandpa coaxed Petie to continue against her will—telling her this was their secret, and that she was special and he loved her best—she suppressed these emotions and their energy remained in her body.

Emotional abuse

Tommy's mother hated her ex-husband, whom six year-old Tommy resembled, and harbored huge resentment towards men in general. Tommy's mother frequently blamed and punished him for anything that went wrong. As a result, he was anxious and sometimes would wet his bed.

After one such bed wetting, Tommy's mother put a diaper on him. She dragged Tommy out into the front yard and ordered Tommy's younger brother to summon Tommy's neighborhood friends. As cars drove by, she had his friends chant: *shame, shame on Tommy*. Afterwards, Tommy could no longer face his friends. His feelings of humiliation, shame and terror were so intense that he disconnected from his emotions, creating massive emotional wounding.

Death of a loved one

Stephanie was four years-old when her older sister, Jamie, died in a car accident. Stephanie had admired Jamie. At the same time she had been envious of Jamie, who was popular and appeared to be her parents' favorite. Stephanie missed her sister terribly and cried every night, sometimes wishing she had been killed instead of her sister. Her parents were overwrought with grief and became emotionally withdrawn. Stephanie falsely interpreted this to mean she was invisible and her parents did not love her. The pain of missing her sister and believing she was unloved was too much for Stephanie to feel.

There are many other possible traumatic events that can accelerate the emotional wounding process, such as bad accidents or illnesses, physical abuse or attempted abortions. Unhealthy environments can also be traumatic, such as growing up with parents who are alcoholics or have personality disorders. Of course, the extent to which any circumstance causes emotional wounding depends upon our unique personalities and the degree to which we personalize our experiences.

CHAPTER 5

CORE WOUNDING

Core wounding

Core wounding is our original wounding and involves suppressed emotions of feeling unloved, unwanted, separate and not enough. It is a seed that gets planted in our unconscious as a result of our personalization of events at a young age when our psyche was immature. It is what begins the process of our believing we are unlovable or not enough. We experience the world through the lens of our core wounding until we unwind its energy. Core wounding can occur over time through repetition of certain situations or behaviors, immediately through a traumatic event, or both.

Monica

Monica was never spanked, hit or yelled at. Her mother was loving, affectionate and gave her lots of attention. From the time Monica was born, she adored her father and longed for his attention. Her dad, however, was indifferent towards her. He walked by her when she was crying, ignored her when she was playing, shut her up with a stern look when she was loud and rarely held her. By the time she was five, Monica was shy, insecure and withdrawn. Her core wound was that she felt inadequate and unworthy of love, especially with regards to men.

Jason

Jason's parents were doting. They frequently hugged and kissed him, and let him know how much they loved him. Jason's father was a successful doctor who worked extensive hours at the hospital. Jason felt a profound separation from his dad and personalized his father's absences to mean he was not important. Many evenings Jason would stare out the window waiting for his father to come home. Mom would explain that dad was busy taking care of people and might be home after bedtime. Jason internalized these messages to mean other people were more important than he was. Even though Jason's parents loved him and treated him well, his core wound, developed over time, was a deep feeling that he was not enough. He continued to feel like a failure even after he became a super-wealthy businessman.

Frank

When Frank was four years old, his father abandoned the family and his grandmother moved in right away. Frank was desperately unhappy and told her he was going to run away. His grandmother responded by packing him a lunch and telling him to go ahead and leave.

As a four year-old he did not sit there and think: *Oh, Dad left because he and Mom aren't getting along, and Grandma is pissed off because she is left to pick up the pieces.* He took it personally and believed he was the reason dad left. Already reeling from this trauma, mom was unavailable and a new caretaker came into his house who he felt wanted to be rid of him. There was no love anywhere. His world fell apart at four years old. His core wound was feeling inadequate and unloved. He unconsciously concluded he did not deserve love and people he loved would go away.

Traumatic events at a young age frequently become core wounds. Therefore, the traumatic events discussed or mentioned in the previous chapter—such as the death of a parent or other loved one, adoption, being the subject of an attempted abortion, emotional abuse, being the recipient or witness of violent behavior or other cruelty, physical accidents, incest or molestation, disease or bad illness—all can be examples of core wounding occurring through an event rather than a process.

Layers of wounding

The simplest visual image of our wounding is that of a mountain. When we look at a mountain sliced in half from top to bottom, we see that it consists of many layers of earth. Each layer consists of different types of earth, and each layer is from a separate time period. Our wounding can be viewed in the same way. Each layer represents a different event where we suppressed some or all of our emotions. The bottom layer is our core wounding. Over time, we add more and more layers on top of our core wounding as we accumulate unfelt emotional energy.

The mountain is a useful visualization for doing Core Emotional Clearing. When we do the work we experience deeper and deeper layers of wounding until we eventually arrive at the bottom layer of our core wounding.

CHAPTER 6

OUR EMOTIONAL WOUNDING CAUSES US TO REJECT OUR REAL SELF AND PROTECT OUR HEART

We conclude there is something wrong with us

As we just saw, when we suppress an emotion we unconsciously draw a false, and negative, conclusion about some aspect of our self. As part of our emotional wounding, therefore, not only do we store emotional energy in our body, but we also unconsciously adopt a negative belief about our self that we associate with that energy.

Emotional wounding is not the only reason we conclude there is something wrong with us. We can also arrive at this conclusion through beliefs others teach us. For example, when we get in trouble for playing in the mud, our joy is made wrong and we may come to believe that what we want is bad. When told we are not hurt when in fact we just fell down and scraped our knee, we may come to believe that we are defective. When we cry because we are in emotional pain, but are told to stop crying because there is nothing to cry about, we learn that we can't trust our feelings and there is something wrong with us.

The more misperceptions of our self we accumulate, the more "evidence" we have collected to substantiate that there really is something wrong with us. These misperceptions are not the result of conscious decisions, but rather are formulated unconsciously.

We protect our heart

When we conclude there is something wrong with us, we make an unconscious decision to protect our heart, our feeling center, which is our love, joy, innocence, purity and authentic self. We do this by hiding who we really are. We also protect our heart by trying not to feel our pain. Of course, even with our most extreme efforts to protect our heart we can only dim, but never completely shut off, our pain just as we cannot completely shut off our love.

Dimming our pain

What we don't realize is we cannot dim our pain without dimming all our other emotions. Our emotions are interconnected: they are a package deal. This means that when we close our heart we also disconnect from our love. This is the most damaging consequence of shutting down our feeling center. We lose our connection with our essence.

The expression "close our heart" does not imply that we shut down our heart completely. We close our heart to varying degrees depending on our personalities, our reactions and the extent of our wounding. There are extreme cases, however, where the trauma has been so great there is a complete disconnection from the self.

Hiding

a. Why we hide

When we believe there is something wrong with us, we develop a fear of showing who we really are. We hide our self because we are scared of being rejected if we reveal our "deficiencies." We hide because we want to avoid the pain of embarrassment or shame surrounding our deficiencies. We also hide when somebody hurts our feelings, such as when we are punished, yelled at, judged, belittled, shamed or hit. Feeling isolated, shy, quiet, inhibited or withdrawn are all symptoms of loss of self. When we hide we are not in our fullest expression. We are not free.

Unless we are completely enlightened, we are hiding some part of our self. Even those who appear all the time to be happy, content and successful can still have insecurities or unresolved feelings of sadness, anger or resentment. We can tell if our heart is completely open when we have no constraints from within—we are free. Until we clear the energy of our emotional wounding, we are not embracing all of our self. Until we acknowledge all of our self, we are at some level living a lie.

b. *The ways we hide*

The way we hide depends on our personality. Some of us dim our light so that we shrink or even disappear. This results in a certain passiveness. We become introverted so as to avoid the spotlight and not be seen. *If I disappear no one can hurt me. If I am quiet no one will judge me or make me wrong. If I don't reveal myself then no one will see my faults and I will be safe and loved.*

Another way to hide is less intuitively obvious: we become aggressive and demanding of attention. We become outgoing and overtly expressive, and may even try to be the "life of the party." This can take the form of seeking an audience: *If I have an audience I must be special. If people are paying attention to me I must be important.* Or it can take a more intimidating form: *I'm going to show you how big and strong I am. I'm going to dominate you and disempower you.*

A-type personalities, for example, are more likely to fall in this second category. They naturally gravitate towards being demonstrative and being seen. Their aggressive behavior, which is often controlling, and their feelings of superiority and arrogance are an over-compensation to counteract feelings of inferiority.

For example, Steven thought he was superior to everybody he met. Steven never wanted a boss and founded his own business. He obsessively built it into a big success, becoming wealthy and well-connected. To people who knew him, he appeared to be a pillar of strength and the model of somebody they wanted on their team because he was confident and dynamic.

The driving force behind Steven's behavior, how-ever, was a sense of inadequacy he developed from his father, who was self-righteous and revered in the world while a tyrant and abuser at home. Steven hired people who couldn't meet his level of intelligence and abilities, thereby bolstering his sense of superiority. At home he was self-righteous when he felt wronged. His behavior was an overcompensation to avoid his feel-ings of inadequacy. His wounding drove him to become professionally successful and wealthy in order to "prove" his greatness to himself and the world.

Though dimming our lights may appear weak and being aggressive may appear strong, both amount to the same: they are different ways of hiding. With one way we fold in our feelings of inadequacy, with the other we push them out.

We close our heart by the age of seven

We have seen how we accumulate emotional wounding. As the wounding mounts, at some point we have collected enough "evidence" to conclude unconsciously that we are inadequate or unlovable—and being our real self is unsafe. This cumulative effect usually has occurred by the age of seven. A traumatic event can produce the same result.

Once our heart is closed

After we close our heart, our subsequent negative experiences provide further "proof" both that closing our heart was a good move and that we need to continue to protect our heart. The following are examples of how we collect this further proof.

Hank

When Hank was thirteen he had a crush on a classmate named Laurie. One night at a party Hank found himself in a side room with her where there were several other kids making out. Hank had never kissed a girl before, but he was very attracted to Laurie and, with others in the room smooching, he felt inspired so he leaned forward and kissed her. She kissed him back, but soon pulled away and exclaimed: *You don't know how to kiss!*

Laurie had thought Hank was experienced and was surprised to discover that he was inept. Hank, however, took it to the extreme and believed Laurie thought he was a dork. He felt a profound humiliation and immediately left not only the room, but also the party. Hank interpreted this incident to be further evidence he was not enough. It took him four years to gather the courage to kiss a girl again.

Nancy

Nancy was attracted to Jonathon during her freshman year of college. One night while hanging out together things heated up and they had sex. She enjoyed the experience and was happy that she had finally lost her virginity. Jonathon, however, left her room early in the morning and then avoided her.

Nancy convinced herself that Jonathon didn't want to see her because she was sexually and personally defective. From this experience she made the decision that she was never going to open herself up again.

When she finally resumed dating, she never let anyone see who she really was and her boyfriends would end up rejecting her. This pattern further reinforced her belief that she was unlovable, inadequate and she had better keep hiding to protect her heart.

George

George was eighteen and sexually active with his girlfriend Maggie. One day Maggie told George she had a male friend coming into town for a month and she did not want to see George during that time period. Whenever he told her he was breaking up with her, she would come over and give him oral sex. During one of these sessions of placation sex, George felt a wave of humiliation. He felt she was treating him like a discardable toy and he was allowing it because he loved the sexual pleasure.

He immediately stopped feeling the pleasure and felt irritation instead. It was in this moment that he unconsciously rejected his sexuality and a dense dark energy lodged in his pubic area. For many years, George rarely dated and, like Nancy, when he did he was so removed that women would leave him. This sealed his belief that he should keep his heart closed to avoid further pain because women were abusive, unstable and untrustworthy.

When we are disconnected from our love, we seek love externally

The more we are disconnected from our love, the more we come to believe there is only one place to find love: from somebody else. As a result, we become needy towards other people. We yearn for others to show us or tell us we are loved. We require others to tell us we're beautiful. We experience a need for praise or adulation to validate that we are worthy, successful or great.

One of the unfortunate results when our partner breaks up with us is that we feel we are devoid of love. Though false, this feeling can result in a sense of devastation. We may also personalize the event, which reinforces our childhood misperception that there is something wrong with us and we are unlovable.

When we search for love externally, love can seem temporary and unsafe. We are on a roller coaster ride, at the mercy of our partner's moods, behaviors and actions. Our sense of well-being becomes volatile as it depends on others. We may come to interpret love as something that abandons us at somebody else's whim. We then associate love with pain because it can go away at any time.

The energetic effects of protecting our heart

Separation from our love

Our authentic self is the energetic light of love that resides in the core of our being. Emotional wounding consists of other energy that acts as a physical barrier, which cuts us off from our love. Depending on our level of disconnection, the color of our wounding can be foggy white, muted grey or even black. The more layers of wounding we have, the darker and denser this energy becomes, and the greater the barrier. Our love cannot move freely if it is blocked. When we dissipate old emotional energy, we remove this barrier and the light of our love can move freely again. This is the main purpose of Core Emotional Clearing.

Separation from our self causes loneliness

People often identify loneliness as being separated from others. That is not loneliness, it is being alone. Many of us have been with a group of friends or in a relationship and still felt lonely. Our feeling of loneliness came from our separation from our self, when we lost contact with our love. Separation from our self is self-abandonment—somebody else did not leave us, we left ourselves. We live in separation from our self, which produces feelings of loneliness.

Depression is caused by depressing our feelings

Depression is the result of depressing our feelings. Visually, it looks like we are holding a lid on top of painful emotions to keep them down. It takes a lot of energy to hold down our pain. The bigger the pain, the more energy it takes to suppress and contain it. We then have less energy available for our everyday life, and can feel listlessness or inertia. When our energy does not move, we feel uncomfortable in our own skin. Separated from our essence, we tend to focus on what is wrong with life and may feel helplessness, hopelessness and despair.

Exceptional events

It is possible through exceptional events to bypass the energy of our emotional wounding and have direct experience of love and joy. Marriage to our beloved, the birth of our child, stunning views of nature, profound intimacy or reunions with loved ones, just to name a few examples, can produce this effect. Unfortunately, without some emotional clearing this effect is temporary. Once the excitement wears off, we are back to feeling the barrier and experiencing through our mind.

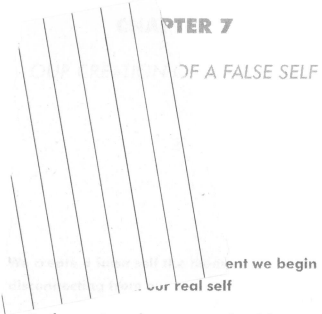

CHAPTER 7

OUR CREATION OF A FALSE SELF

We create a false self the moment we begin disconnecting from our real self

In the previous chapter we explored how we reject, and disconnect from, our real self. By doing this we are at the same time creating a false self.

Absent trauma, we begin our life free. Our light is shining. We are uninhibited, unafraid and undoubting. We are our fullest expression of love and joy. As we have seen, it is part of the human condition to have emotional wounding and develop beliefs that there is something wrong with us. As soon as this begins, the physical barrier of our emotional wounding masks and constricts our clear, bright, yellow-white light. Once our light is masked, we are disconnected to some extent from our essence. The very act of shutting down to any degree means that we are being false. When we are disconnected from our self, we cannot be who we are. We become who we are not.

We are creating our false self. Absent traumatic events, this is generally a gradual process that occurs in response to whatever events happen in our daily life.

We also create a false self by trading inauthentic behavior for acceptance and love

What the trade is

We also create a false self as an attempt to satisfy our fundamental psychological need to feel loved. As we saw in the previous chapter, the more we close our heart, the more we disconnect from our love. That leaves only one other place to find love: the external world. When we reject our real self, however, presenting it to the world seems like a bad idea. We unconsciously implement damage control by hiding our real self and replacing it with something we feel others will find more appealing. We become what we believe others want us to be, modifying our behavior and beliefs according to the situations and people we encounter. The more aspects of our self we reject, the more extensive a false self we create.

How the trade happens

There is no set blueprint for trading inauthentic behavior for love because the trade happens in response to the particular events of our life. Beginning at an early age, we try different strategies and settle on the ones that will get us what we believe is love. We associate attention with love, even if it is negative attention.

The common feature is the following pattern: we are being our authentic self; we receive a reaction from others; we internalize the reaction to mean it is not all right to be ourselves; and we then try to become what we believe will get us acceptance.

Dirk

Dirk's mom went to work when he was six weeks old and would return late at night. His father also worked and did not spend any significant time with him. Dirk was left alone in his crib with babysitters as caretakers. Dirk internalized the abandonment to mean he was being rejected because he was not enough. When he was a toddler, Dirk's reaction was to try to be blindly obedient so that his parents would not go away. He unconsciously feared that if he upset them they would leave and never come back.

Margaret

Margaret's mother learned through a book that it is good to let a baby cry because it developed the baby's lungs and prevented the baby from developing manipulative habits. Margaret's mother regularly let her cry herself to sleep. So there often was no response when Margaret would scream because she was hungry, cold, upset, soiled or in pain. Margaret "learned" that her primal needs were unimportant—and that she was unimportant. Her needs, wants and desires were wrong. As a toddler she realized that she could get her mother's attention by doing things her mother didn't want her to do. The false self she created was belligerent and rebellious.

Jack

As a two-year-old, Jack wanted to explore every inch of the house. Whenever he would unroll the toilet paper, smear his mother's lipstick or climb into precarious positions, his parents would yell at him, spank him or imprison him in his crib. When he expressed his disappointment through a tantrum, he got into trouble for that too. Jack internalized his parents' anger to mean they did not love him and that his curiosity and creativity were bad—he was bad. He soon squelched his sense of adventure. Later he discovered that being humorous made his parents laugh and embrace him.

Over time, he realized that most people love to laugh. Humor became his disguise and an overcompensation to avoid being rejected.

Paula

Paula's grandpa would effusively express his love by telling her he loved her more than anybody else. Paula took these declarations to mean that nobody else loved her, especially her mother. In order to gain love, she insisted on helping mom with everything. *I'll get it. I can do it for you. I'll help you.* She also interpreted her mother's absences as abandonment and asked mom to stay home instead of going to work. When her mother responded she needed to work so they could eat, Paula stopped eating so that mom could stay with her.

Julie

Julie's mom was slender and beautiful whereas Julie was a stocky plain-looking little girl. Mom would buy clothes that were too small for Julie as an incentive for her daughter to lose weight. Julie unconsciously concluded that she was defective and God had made her wrong. As a five-year-old she tried to lose weight to please her mom, but realized she'd never look like mom. She did discover, however, that mom reacted more warmly to her when she was chipper and positive. It became her predominant trait to look only at the bright side of any situation and refuse to acknowledge anything negative. To this day, she still will not look into a mirror.

Brad

Brad was painting pictures with his new finger paint set. When he became tired of painting, he showed his artwork to his father, who said: Wow, that is so beautiful! Nice job! Though Brad no longer felt like painting, he went back to his room and painted five more pictures because he wanted more attention from his dad. His motivation was no longer personal joy, but to get more love.

Other unconscious strategies could be: *I'll be loved if–*

- ❤ *I hide my hatred for my little brother;*

- ❤ *I only hit my sister when mom isn't looking;*

- ❤ *I put on a smiley face to keep mom happy;*

- ❤ *I downplay my joy so dad will be comfortable;*

- ❤ *I don't disagree with anyone;*

- ❤ *I tell you what you want to hear;*

- ❤ *I'm invisible;*

- ❤ *I throw a tantrum so mom will pay attention;*

- 💜 *I'm the life of the party;*

- 💜 *I like the same things you do;*

- 💜 *I excel in school and become a doctor or lawyer;*

- 💜 *I marry who my parents want me to;*

- 💜 *I'm thin;*

- 💜 *I wear a certain designer's clothes or shoes.*

We veer further and further away from our real self as we learn to navigate life by living inauthentically in return for acceptance or love.

A by-product of our false self is that it helps us feel less pain

We don't like to feel pain for the simple reason that it hurts and is uncomfortable. Facing and feeling very deep emotions can be frightening. Furthermore, our reptilian brain "fight or flight" response is activated by threat. Threat includes pain, both emotional and physical: emotional pain is physically painful. As we have seen, we carry the energy of our emotional wounding inside us. When we feel this energy, we feel pain. As a result, we have strong unconscious drives that steer us away from feeling our emotional wounding.

When we disconnect from our self and protect our heart, we cannot feel as strongly. Consequently, our false identity supports our unconscious drives to feel less pain.

We generate thoughts to distract us from our pain

Another by-product of our false identity is that we generate thoughts. Once we have emotional wounding, there is a barrier that prevents the light of our love from moving with complete freedom. We are no longer completely authentic. Our emotional body has awareness that something is wrong because we feel discomfort. We are not consciously aware that the discomfort is from our wounding; rather we simply want to get rid of the discomfort because it is uncomfortable.

Our brain tries to identify what is causing the discomfort. As the energy of our wounding is part of our unconscious, however, it is impossible for our logical mind to figure out the cause. Though our mind never stops this quest, at some stage we discover distraction as a Plan B. If we can't make the discomfort go away, we do the next best thing: distract.

Thoughts are a powerful distraction from feeling our discomfort. By occupying our attention, our thoughts prevent us from fully experiencing the present—which includes feeling our emotions. As we shall explore in detail in the next chapter, the most potent distracters are fearful thoughts because fear naturally dominates our attention.

For example, Connie would sometimes spin stories about her boyfriend leaving her or becoming involved with another woman. Other times she would remember past experiences with her father where she felt she had disappointed him. These thoughts would cause her to feel grief and sometimes even cry in despair. These thoughts would feed on themselves and perpetuate further suffering.

By spinning these stories, Connie in effect was trading feeling a more familiar mind-generated pain for feeling her discomfort. If she were completely in the present, she would feel her discomfort, which represented a mystery because her mind cannot figure it out. We tend to choose the familiar over the unknown.

Though fearful thoughts act as the most powerful distractions, all thoughts serve as distractions. The thoughts we generate may be mundane, such as crafting to-do lists, or they may have elements of pleasure, such as creating a fantasy about something we enjoy or want. Thoughts that do not create fear are no less imaginary than fearful thoughts and serve the same purpose of distracting ourselves from feeling our discomfort in the present.

Using Connie as an example again, sometimes she would daydream about being a singer or a dancer or someone famous. These thoughts would create feelings of joy, excitement and elation at feeling special and loved. Just as when she was a child, she lived in a fantasy world. These thoughts gave her something to occupy her focus and distract her from feeling how uncomfortable she felt within herself. Her thoughts served as a way to avoid facing herself.

Sometimes we go to the extreme of using our thoughts to make ourselves physically ill in order to avoid our discomfort. For example, Carol worried constantly about everything: her children, the legal system, her neighbors, the country's morality, the deficiencies of the next generation, the economy, having enough money, terrorism, human stupidity, overpopulation, everybody else's drama. Her constant worrying created dis-ease in the form of ulcers and high blood pressure. Carol was so reluctant to look inside herself that she was willing to trade getting sick for feeling the discomfort of her wounding.

Our false identity is not who we are—it is who we have come to believe we are

Our false identity is how we have come to identify ourselves. It is important to realize that our false identity is not a separate part of us. Rather, though our false identity is not who we really are, it is still our identity. It is who we have come to believe we are. As we create our false identity, the truth of who we really are becomes more and more elusive.

CHAPTER 8

FEAR THAT WE CREATE – A PROMINENT EFFECT OF OUR FALSE IDENTITY

One of the primary ways our false identity shields us from pain is to generate fear. Because of our reptilian brain "fight or flight" instincts, fear is the emotion that gets priority attention. Fear consumes and immobilizes us. When we are stuck in fear, we are unable to feel our other emotions.

The shocks and traumas we carry in our body cause us to feel fear

Whatever shocks and traumas we experienced as part of our emotional wounding remain inside us. These energies are still lodged in the cells of our body.

Consequently, we physically carry these shocks and traumas—and the associated fear—around with us.

It is the nature of our false identity to generate fear

Once we make the unconscious decision that there is something wrong with us, we fear that who we are is not enough. We become afraid to be seen. We fear expressing ourselves. We fear asking for what we want. We fear being rejected. We fear we won't find love—and if we do find it we fear it can disappear at any time.

Our mind creates fear by spinning threatening stories

Our mind distracts us from our emotions by inventing stories that generate fear based on an imagined threat that is not actually occurring. Whether or not we take steps to avoid this "threat," we will still be safe because the threat is imaginary. Yet, we still react fearfully. It is similar to feeling fear in a movie in that we feel the fear, but it is not related to a real danger because we are sitting in a safe cinema and the movie consists of images on a screen.

Example of imagined physical danger

Using an example involving fear for our physical safety, I was with a dear friend of mine, Bob, back-packing in the Alaska wilderness. We were traveling on foot through an area known to have grizzly bears. As we embarked on our journey, there were no bears in sight. We were, of course, highly justified in being cautious given the potential appearance of bears and the many reported attacks on humans. This definitely influenced our strategy: we sought to avoid the bears' favorite spots and had a rifle ready in order to protect ourselves. Without any bears in sight, however, there was no real current danger and, therefore, no reason to feel fear.

Nevertheless, during the journey Bob's mind kept spinning stories that a bear would suddenly appear out of nowhere. These stories generated continual fear and anxiety inside him. He played out many scenarios of what he would do "if" it happened. We did not come across any bears. As a result of his thoughts, however, Bob felt fear throughout the entire journey. Because of the nature of fear, it dominated his attention. Despite having encountered no real danger, he was an emotional wreck by the end of the journey as a result of the stories his mind created. By listening to his mind, he missed out on our time together and the incredible beauty of Alaska.

Example of imagined psychological threat

The same dynamic is involved when we create fear of an imagined psychological, rather than physical, threat. Paul went to a party where he knew only the host, who was too busy to spend time with him. Even though Paul wanted to meet new people, he feared introducing himself. His mind, like a broken record, kept spinning a story that if he introduced himself to others he would be exposed as being boring and stupid, and he would be judged.

The net result was that Paul ended up alone in the corner of the room, just watching and drinking. His story of rejection dominated his behavior—even though he never actually faced a situation where he might be rejected.

Taking ourselves down

Just as our mind spins stories about imagined threats, our mind also spins stories that highlight our perceived inadequacies. As these stories focus on what we falsely believe to be our flaws, they amplify our fears and anxieties. I call this taking ourselves down.

Shari

Shari had been close to Mike's parents and had great respect for them. After she broke up with Mike, however, all communication with his parents stopped. Shari began imagining that Mike's parents criticized how she had treated him. So even though Mike's parents still thought very highly of her, Shari's mind was creating imaginary criticism. As a result, she was in a continual state of anxiety over her behavior during the relationship. Shari was taking herself down in a manner consistent with her misperceptions of her inadequacies—and nobody else was involved.

Joe

Joe was a home inspector who made a mistake with an inspection. The woman who owned the house was furious with Joe and called him names. That night Joe woke up at three in the morning and could not get back to sleep. His mind kept spinning over and over the same story about how he had messed up: he was incompetent and had let the woman down. Joe was taking himself down. He was on the mind train, spinning stories about how he could not do things right and how he could not please women.

The fears we create in our mind are a mirage

Through our mind we spin stories of imaginary dangers and criticisms so habitually that we usually are not even aware we are doing it. Once we become conscious that we are inventing these stories, we notice the frequency with which we create them and how relentlessly distracting they can be.

These "dangers" and "criticisms" are a mirage. The "situations" are purely the creation of our own thoughts. We invent them—they have no basis in reality. The fear our mind generates is a cage of our own making in which we become trapped. We do this to ourselves.

We become susceptible to fear-inducing messages

One of the many unfortunate results of continual exposure to fear is that we come to resonate with it. Fear becomes the emotion we relate and react to the most. This makes us more susceptible to fear-based messages and threats. We become more prone to being persuaded by messages that arouse fear and are more easily controlled when fear is waved at us.

Our upbringing can reinforce our fears

Our tendency to feel fear is heightened if we were brought up with fear as a motivator. *Wait 'til your father gets home.* It was instilled in us that if we are disobedient or break the rules then we'll be punished or go to hell. Whether the motivation was to protect us or to control us, we were taught to be afraid. As a result, we learned to react to life with fear and anxiety.

We fear our pain

Almost no one enjoys feeling emotional pain. We have a natural tendency to avoid feeling anything that hurts. This tendency is exacerbated when we get into the habit of suppressing our feelings, which causes us to gradually lose our facility to feel them. We then become even more afraid to feel our pain and convince ourselves it is not necessary to do so. This fear causes us to continue to look at pain from a child's perspective.

We come to identify with our fears

As we have seen, our false identity is not who we are, but who we have come to think we are. As our fears are part of our false identity, we wrongly believe that our fears are part of who we really are. We become attached to this misperception of our self, thereby perpetuating our own suffering.

CHAPTER 9

OTHER NEGATIVE EFFECTS
OF OUR FALSE IDENTITY

Besides the creation of fear, our false identity can have many other harmful effects. The greater our separation from our self and the more extensive a false identity we create, the more likely we are to have the following tendencies:

Difficulty being with ourselves: Many of us find it difficult to be with ourselves because our body carries so much discomfort from our emotional wounding. We feel this discomfort the strongest when we are idle. When we have a certain level of unease in our body, we feel propelled to do some activity in excess—for example, eat, drink, smoke, go for a ride, watch television, have sex, gossip, do sports, daydream, shop, cook, clean, gamble—which distracts us from that discomfort. While these activities may be a healthy normal part of life, when we are obsessed or driven they can be a way to avoid facing and feeling our emotions.

The greater our pain, the more powerful is our compulsion to distract ourselves. This is the trademark of the 'holics (alcoholics, shopaholics, sexaholics, workaholics, "gamblaholics"). We might believe ourselves to be easily bored, or we might resist the idea of spending time alone or having nothing specific to do. The compulsion to distract ourselves is a sign of great wounding. We seek a powerful force to divert our attention.

Inability to live in the present: Put another way, the discomfort, or even turmoil, we carry in our body from our emotional wounding makes it uncomfortable for us to be in the moment. Our impulse to "do something," or have our mind thoughts occupy our attention, prevents us from living fully in the present. We run hard and fast from our emotions. The more emotional wounding we have stored in our body, the more the discomfort makes living in the present seem like a bad idea.

Inability to listen to our inner knowing: The less present we are, the less we are able to sense our inner knowing, robbing us of invaluable guidance.

Less connection to our "feel good" emotions: As we have seen, our efforts to dull our painful emotions also result in the dulling of our pleasurable emotions.

Attraction to external stimulus: The dulling of our emotions has a further consequence: we need greater and more intense external stimulus in order to feel. We are attracted to activities that produce adrenaline which pierces our protective numbing, such as extreme sports, racing, war and "trauma drama" relationships. Many movies and video games are packed with over-the-top stimulus. Sexual perversion is another indication of a need for intense stimulation in order to overcome numbing.

Lack of comfort with success: We might have a lack of ease with success, believing we did not deserve it. For example, if we are accepted to a good school we might have thoughts such as: *they're going to find out I'm the mistake*, or if we win a prize: *they're going to discover I'm a fraud.* In extreme cases, we may not even seek success because we believe we are not capable and don't want to be disappointed.

We are emotionally stuck at the level of maturity where we shut down: Until we clear our emotional wounds, we remain stuck at the age where we shut down. After this time, we react in the same manner and from the same perspective as when we were that age. For example, Peter was a sixty-nine-year-old former Special Forces soldier, martial arts expert and body-guard. At a get-together at his house one of his close friends borrowed a quilt to lie down on. When Peter noticed, he yelled: *That's my blanket! I don't want anybody touching my blanket!* He grabbed a book and tossed it at his friend, saying: *You might as well take this too.*

Increased compliancy: The more we believe there is something wrong with us, the more we doubt ourselves and are more inclined to believe what others tell us. As a result, we become more accommodating at the expense of our true self.

Overcompensating behavior: We feel we need to help others in order to be appreciated and accepted. This may take the form of excessive caretaking or making the needs of others more important than our own. At the extreme, we may seek to create the illusion that we are vital and necessary for the well-being of a group, community or even all of humanity. Our creation of this illusion is an overcompensation to avoid deep-seated feelings of inadequacy.

Loss of altruism: When we help people because of our love, we help them simply because they need help. This altruism is lost when we seek importance, status, acceptance or love in exchange for our good deeds.

Celebrity fixation: Focusing on celebrities is another way we avoid our own experience. We follow the lives of "stars" by reading about them and watching their stories on television. We want to be like them because they receive so much attention and adulation. We seek to replace the dullness, unhappiness and inadequacy we feel in our life by living vicariously through people we perceive to be special, loved and glamorous.

Inability to receive compliments: We are uncomfortable when others say nice things about us. We downplay or deflect compliments because we do not believe we are worthy or that we matter.

Loss of ability to express ourselves: When we believe there is something wrong with us we do not feel free to express ourselves because we fear that revealing who we are will show others our inadequacies. We also have difficulty expressing what we want. Instead of being open and direct, we either fail to express what we want or we become more prone to roundabout statements or even manipulation.

Projection of self-abandonment onto others: Our self-rejection causes separation from our self. In effect, we abandon ourselves. We tend to project this self-abandonment onto others. We experience the behaviors of others to mean that they are abandoning us. For example, Michele's body would become uncomfortable every time her husband left to run errands or have a drink with the boys. It didn't matter that her husband spent virtually all of his free time with her. Every time he left her she felt abandoned.

People leave us: When people go away they are sometimes responding to the energy of our wounding, which is our inauthentic self. On an unconscious level they can feel that we are not being our entire self (even though they also may be hiding who they are!). They want to be with the real us, and become frustrated when they cannot feel our real self. People leave because they don't like the false self we present and resent that we will not give them our heart and share who we really are.

Punishing others: The more we close our heart, the more we become insensitive, vengeful and hurtful. When we feel hurt or disappointed, our knee-jerk reaction is to hurt back. We may unconsciously become angry and seek to punish. This punishment often takes the form of withholding our love. People want to feel our love, so when we withhold it we hurt them.

Blaming others: Blaming others is a diversion. It hides who we are. By keeping the focus on somebody else, we avoid being seen and being vulnerable. By blaming others we also avoid facing our feelings. In this way, we avoid having to revisit old feelings of pain, shame, embarrassment or humiliation that we have come to dread. By its very nature, this tendency is a fundamental roadblock to healing.

Seeing ourselves as victims: We create situations that reflect and substantiate our beliefs. The net result is that our negative beliefs about our self, which arise from our misinterpretation of events, cause us to have bad experiences. This pattern reinforces our misperception that we are inadequate and life works against us. It becomes a vicious cycle. Ironically, though we create this vicious cycle, we tend to draw the opposite conclusion—that there's nothing we can do about it: bad things just happen to us, we are jinxed, we have no control over our life, we are victims.

One of the biggest problems with adopting a victim mentality is that it causes us to give away our power. We become prone to blaming others for what happens to us. We come to believe that power, including power over our lives, lies in the external world and we have no control over what happens to us.

There is evidence of this victim mind set wherever we look. For example, we see it in many relationships, where blaming can be rampant. We see it in the disempowering language many people use: *Why do people always leave me? Why can't I catch a break? Why is this happening to me? What have I done wrong? I must be bad and God's punishing me.* An example at a societal level is our litigation society. If we pour scalding coffee over ourselves then we must sue whoever gave us the coffee because it's that person's fault.

People who believe themselves to be the biggest victims, and who are the biggest whiners and blamers, often have dense black energy throughout their body, indicating lots of wounding and a lack of consciousness.

Creating the illusion of superiority

Many of us overcompensate for our sense of weakness and inadequacy by feeling superior. Whether through money, status, job prestige, knowledge, intelligence, looks or some other external measure, we seek to show that we are better than others. We want to be able to point to our qualities, education or "success" that "prove" we are better. We want to demonstrate to ourselves and others that we are worthy rather than deficient.

Feeling superior creates more separation

One of the ways we try to create the illusion of superiority is to categorize and then declare the category in which we place ourselves to be better. The more categories we make, the more instances of "superiority" we create. And for good measure, we might also deem people in other categories to be not just inferior but also deficient.

So our country is better and the citizens of certain other countries are low-lives. Our ethnic group is the best and the members of certain other groups are stupid—and evil because their goal in life is to harm us. The adherents of our religion are going to heaven and the heathen followers of other religions are going to hell. The students from our university are the most gifted and the students from other universities are weenies. The people in our neighborhood are more special than the ones with the smaller houses in the next neighborhood.

The meaning we make of these categorizations is clearly specious. Most of us have never even lived in another country, become close to many people of other ethnic groups or religions, attended even one other university or known many people of other economic classes. Through our self-serving categorizations all we have created is the illusion of superiority.

The one real thing we have created is yet more separation. The by-product of separating from our self is separating from others as well. With each categorization we succeed in separating ourselves from more and more people, thereby reducing the number of people we view as eligible for connection to us. Through our false identity we have yet again created more isolation.

Our feeling of superiority is a reflection of our wounding, not our specialness.

The journey away from our real self is unavoidable

In case we become discouraged reading about all the effects of our false identity, it is important to realize that the journey away from our self is part of the human experience. There is no way for us to avoid it—we all create a false identity. Of course, some of us will reject more aspects of our self than others and, therefore, will create a more extensive false identity.

CHAPTER 10

OUR FALSE IDENTITY
IS A POOR COPING MECHANISM

It is impossible to feel love from others

Trading inauthentic behavior for love is a doomed strategy because seeking love externally will not help us feel love. When we feel love, it does not come from another person. To better understand, let's look at the example of a friend cutting his or her hand. If we have not had a similar experience, we cannot relate to it. But even if we have, we still cannot feel our friend's pain. Rather, we are operating off of our memory of feeling our own pain from a similar event. We can relate to somebody else's pain, but we cannot actually feel somebody else's pain.

Similarly, we cannot actually feel somebody else's love. We can relate to it, however, because of our experience of feeling our own love. When we receive love from somebody else, we feel love not because we feel that person's love, but rather because we know what our love feels like. The warmth and joy we feel at receiving love is coming from inside of us. We're not getting it from out there. When our heart is closed we cannot feel love because we are blocking our connection to our love, not somebody else's love.

The great irony is that the more we create a false self in order to feel love, the more we deprive ourselves of feeling love. We disconnect from our love, which we otherwise would be able to feel, and instead seek love from the outside, which is impossible for us to feel.

Our misguided search for love from others becomes even more misguided when we misidentify "love." We tend to identify love with the attention we received growing up. That became our template for "love," whether our family was functional or dysfunctional. The messages from our caretakers act as programming which cuts a groove in our psyche that this is love. If inaccurate, the template can wreak havoc with our perception of love.

Our false identity is built on false foundations

Our false identity does not represent the truth of who we are. It is built upon false beliefs:

The false belief that it is best to avoid feeling our pain

Because we tend to associate a negative self-belief with the energy of our wounding, feeling our pain reminds us of our perceived inadequacies. In addition, we have learned from others that it is inappropriate to feel certain emotions. Indeed, we live in a society that discourages feeling pain and many of us believe we are unable to cope with our feelings. We also may have learned that other people do not want to be around us when we are in pain. We respond by not going there.

Suppressing our emotions, however, is completely counterproductive. When we suppress our emotions not only do we prevent ourselves from healing, but we also add to our emotional wounding. The most counterproductive consequence of shutting down our heart is that we also shut down our connection to our love within. What we think will protect us actually causes us enormous harm.

The false belief that we are unlovable

Our essence is love. We only feel "unlovable" when our wounding is a barrier to our love. Our love, however, is always there. We are merely disconnected from it. But we always have the ability to reconnect to our love by unwinding the energy of our emotional wounding—we are always lovable.

We developed our false identity when we had an immature perspective

Our false identity is a primitive coping mechanism developed during our emotional immaturity. As our false identity operates under false premises that sabotage our interests, our false identity serves as a remarkably poor caretaker of our well-being.

Core Emotional Clearing unwinds our emotional wounding and dissolves our false identity

We cannot simply discipline our thoughts in order to "get over" our emotional wounding. Similarly, nothing outside of us—whether "success," accomplishments, status, sex, job, house or money—can impact our emotional wounding. Mere talk also will not rid us of this wounding. Though talk may lead to increased awareness, and awareness is the important first step in the healing process, awareness alone will not heal us. All of these approaches operate through the mind, so none of these approaches affects the energy of our wounding. Until we unwind this energy, our wounding remains lodged in our body and we are at the mercy of our unconscious.

We clear the energy of our wounding by going inside and feeling our unfelt emotions. Now that we understand the dynamics of emotional energy and wounding, we are ready to learn about Core Emotional Clearing.

PART II

THE JOURNEY BACK TO OUR SELF

He who looks outside
dreams,
he who looks inside
wakes.

Carl Jung

SECTION A

TRIGGERS –
HOW WE ACCESS THE ENERGY
OF OUR EMOTIONAL WOUNDING

CHAPTER 11

TRIGGERS: HOW WE ACCESS THE UNFELT EMOTIONS STORED IN OUR UNCONSCIOUS

Triggers are our guide to accessing our unfelt emotions

While feeling our unfelt emotions is the centerpiece of Core Emotional Clearing, our first task is to access them. The unfelt emotions of our core wounds have been in our body a very long time and are sometimes so deeply buried that we are not even aware of their existence.

This raises the question: how do we access our unfelt emotions? What we need is a portal to the past, a gateway to our stored emotional energy, a guide into our unconscious. This guide is what I will call a "trigger." When we are triggered we have an opportunity to access our unfelt emotions.

How to recognize we are being triggered

We are triggered when we react to a situation or thought by feeling a zing or blast of energy that gives us the sensation of being lit up. We become defensive, blaming, angry or sad. Without knowing what triggers are, some people might refer to this as "having our buttons pushed." The intensity of our reaction is greater than the situation warrants.

Visual triggers

Alec saw a parent grab and hit a child. He immediately felt a sharp rush of anger zoom through his chest.

Twelve-year-old Zan saw her older sisters being scolded by her mother. She fled, filled with anguish, and hid the rest of the day.

While watching the concentration camp guard in *Schindler's List* get up in the morning and from his balcony shoot a prisoner for fun, Chris experienced a sharp burst of fear as his chest tightened.

Pat saw animals on television being abused and felt a sickening pain inside.

Peter, a lawyer, watched a judge demean another lawyer for sport and felt a twisting anxiety gnaw at his stomach.

Alice would shudder when she encountered older men with a beard dressed in jeans because that was the look of the man who had molested her.

Verbal triggers

Bill was at a family function and flirted with a woman to whom he was sexually attracted. After the function, a family friend told Bill that the way he had talked to the woman was inappropriate. Bill instantly became belligerent and defensive.

Patrick complained to Meredith that since she wasn't working he was shouldering the entire financial burden. Meredith immediately became angry and stormed out of the room, screaming at Patrick that he was making her feel guilty and unappreciated.

Sharon was putting on a surprise birthday play for her fiancé, using friends as actors. At the party she tried to get the friends to rehearse, but they told her they wanted to get back to the party. Sharon started to cry.

At the end of a cocktail party, Philip raved to his bride-to-be, Patricia, about the glass of vintage port a friend had served him. Patricia chastised Philip for not calling her over to share in the port. Patricia was not the only one triggered: Philip tossed and turned all night, filled with anxiety.

How triggers act as a guide

When we are triggered, we are having a reaction to something outside of us that is touching something inside of us. More specifically, we are having a reaction in the present to unfelt emotions from our past. A current emotion (the triggered emotion) is lighting up the energy of an emotional wound already stored in our body.

The triggered emotion acts as a conduit by connecting to an old, unfelt emotion. As we shall see later in detail, after we completely feel the triggered emotion an unfelt emotion will be revealed, thereby giving us another chance to feel that unfelt emotion and clear ourselves of its energy.

The "reason" for the connection between a triggered emotion and a stored unfelt emotion may be obvious

We previously encountered the example where Alec saw a parent grab and hit a child, and in response he felt a sharp rush of anger. Alec had been physically abused when young and witnessing the scene lit up unfelt emotions of insignificance, fear and shame.

We also saw the example of Bill becoming belligerent when accused of inappropriate flirtation. As a child Bill's father shamed him around his sexuality. Over time, Bill came to believe that his sexual impulses were bad and there was something wrong with him. His reaction came from the lighting up of old unfelt emotions of shame and inadequacy buried deep inside him.

The "reason" for the connection between a triggered emotion and a stored unfelt emotion may not be obvious

Bracken would become highly agitated whenever he and his wife, Faye, would discuss buying a house. Bracken always thought that he became so upset because he felt they couldn't afford a house. When he finally directed his attention inward at the triggered anger, it eventually turned into a profound sadness. A memory popped up of when he was twelve years old: his mother wanted him to stand up to his vicious father for her and she would withhold her love if he refused.

The two situations seemed entirely different, but had the same emotional charge. In Bracken's mind, each woman wanted him to do something for her that he felt incapable of doing: Faye wanted him to buy a house and his mother wanted him to fight dad. And he believed each withheld love if he failed to comply. Being triggered over buying a house was Bracken's doorway to his suppressed feelings of being used and victimized.

We don't need to know the "reason" for the connection between the triggered emotion and our old emotional wound

It is critical to keep in mind that in order to do Core Emotional Clearing we don't need to know or understand the link between the present triggered emotion and the stored unfelt emotion. The triggered emotion will automatically connect us to where we need to go. There is nothing for us to figure out—no thought or analysis or logic is required.

Triggers are about our past

The trigger examples also illustrate that being triggered is about us and our past. We do not have the strong reaction of a trigger unless we have experienced an event that made us feel hurt in some similar way. Because we did not completely feel the emotional pain at the time it occurred, we still carry with us the energy of what it feels like to be treated that way.

Absent similar emotional wounding, we would simply say to ourselves: *that's inappropriate* or *that's hurtful,* but we would not have the same strong burst of energy zipping through us. This is true even in extreme cases. For example, we can see violent war footage and, absent a resonant emotional wound, we will not react in a deeply emotional way. We may empathize, but we will not be triggered.

Triggers are the essential first step to Core Emotional Clearing

Triggers play an essential role in our Core Emotional Clearing. They are the "missing link" that enables us to gain access to unfelt emotions that are buried in our unconscious. They are the critical first step that launches our Core Emotional Clearing. Through the triggered emotion, we have another opportunity to feel an emotion that we previously suppressed.

CHAPTER 12

A DIFFERENT TYPE OF TRIGGER: JUDGMENTS AND MIRRORING

Judging others is how we externalize our self-judgment

Our misperceptions that we are not enough are a form of self-judgment. The more we separate from our self, the more we project our internal life onto the external world. Making our self-judgments about other people is simply another form of externalizing our internal experiences. We come to see in others the aspects of our self we have rejected: other people become our mirror.

The more we reject our self, the more we reject the external world, causing us to become more judgmental. Then we look for what is wrong in life. We can even think that the world is unsafe and that people in general are stupid, bad or incompetent.

Judgments of others are triggers

Though we tend to think our judgments are about others, judging is actually another form of triggering. The energetic charge of triggering accompanies every judgment we make. From an energy perspective, it is an illusion that judgments are about the person we are judging. Like any other trigger, the energetic significance is that the energy of an old emotional wound has been lit up and we have an opportunity to heal. A trigger is a trigger.

Betty's judgment of Janna's promiscuity

Betty judged Janna as being a promiscuous whore. She noticed her judgment was charged with angry thoughts: *she just wants to use men, she just wants attention, she's a slut*. Betty even felt that Janna had no right to live. Betty had been triggered.

Her judgment did not have anything to do with Janna or sex. Betty was shy and withdrawn. She generally felt her dreams were out of her reach and tended to shy away from going after what she wanted. Betty had unresolved emotional pain that she had lost years of her life by hiding and never feeling the freedom to express who she really was. Her judgment was related to her own suffocated sense of despair. Though Betty was happily married and had no interest in having an affair, Janna's confidence and aggressive pursuit of what she wanted triggered Betty.

Sherry's judgment of Frank's neediness

Sherry judged Frank as being extremely needy. He was always pulling on her and seeking attention. When Frank got clingy, Sherry became irritated and sometimes angry. Sherry was triggered because Frank was mirroring aspects of herself that she had not yet embraced. Growing up, she was around big energies that made her feel weak and incapable. When Frank was needy, Sherry saw the powerless part of herself, which disgusted her.

Jake's judgment of his wife's insecurities

Jake was a really nice guy and an extremely successful businessman. He was vivacious, gregarious, successful, open and at ease talking to both friends and strangers. Jake often judged his wife Martha as being angry and attacking. Although the judgment was accurate, what Martha was reflecting back to Jake was his own suppressed anger. Since Jake rejected his own anger, he judged hers.

Chelsea's judgment of Mark's inability to stand up for himself

When Mark reacted to Chelsea's aggressive behavior by shutting down emotionally, she judged him to be spineless. Mark was mirroring Chelsea's self-judgment that she was inadequate. Chelsea had deep emotional wounds over her father's prolonged physical and emotional absences when she was growing up. So Mark's becoming emotionally unavailable would light up her unfelt emotions of insignificance related to her father.

The unfortunate bias against judging

Because our society disapproves of judgments, most people won't admit that they have them—even though people are judging all the time. This is a pity because negating our judgments deprives us of healing opportunities.

The antisocial part of judging is expressing the judgment to the person we are judging, thereby hurting that person's feelings. In order to do Core Emotional Clearing, however, we do not need to express our judgment to the person we are judging. We only need to feel the emotion behind the judgment, which we can do on our own. So when we use a judgment as a healing tool—where our entire experience of the emotions behind the judgment is internal—the judgment is both welcome and constructive. Once we realize that the judgment is really about us, we no longer need to feel awkward about having a judgment.

CHAPTER 13

THE GOLDEN RULE OF TRIGGERS:
TRIGGERS ARE ABOUT US

A trigger is about our emotional wounding

We are now ready for one of the simplest, yet most powerful, principles of Core Emotional Clearing. Though we have already encountered this principle in our discussion of triggers, it is so important it requires its own chapter. Despite its simplicity, this is the principle that we tend to find the most difficult to understand at an intuitive level and incorporate into our lives:

Every time we are triggered, the triggered emotion is about an old emotional wound that already resides within us.

Put another way, whenever we are triggered it is about what is happening inside us. Each time we get triggered, this is a signal that we have access to an unfelt emotion stored within.

The flip side is that being triggered is <u>not</u> about anything outside of us, such as the person or situation triggering us. This is precisely why the triggered emotion is stronger than the present situation warrants: the overreaction is attributable to old unfelt emotions that have been lit up.

Marty

Marty became infuriated when another driver cut him off. He drove in front of the other car, tore his door open and jumped out. Suddenly, he asked himself: *what are you doing?*

His question arose not from the standpoint that his behavior was crazy or inappropriate (which it was), but from his awareness that the anger surging through his body was so much bigger than the incident warranted. This was not about the other driver. It was during this incident that Marty viscerally woke up to the truth that his reactions are about him, and not about how the world was mistreating him.

The current issue is never the issue

Any current issue that triggers us is not the real issue. It is our portal to the real issue—the energy of our emotional wounding has been lit up. Whatever triggered us is irrelevant to what is happening energetically.

Teresa

Teresa's lover, Paul, went on a weekend trip with his longtime platonic friend, Mary. When Teresa found out, she was intensely triggered. She became consumed with jealousy, believing that Paul and Mary were having sex.

Teresa's triggering was not about Paul and Mary's trip. The incident in the present lit up her old emotional wounding surrounding jealousy of her sister. When Teresa was a little girl she believed her father neglected her and gave his love to her sister instead. Jealousy was a yoke that had surrounded her for as long as she could remember. This is why Teresa's reaction to her boyfriend being away on a platonic trip with another woman was so intense.

Alice

Alice really wanted to have a house, children and be a stay-at-home mom. Her false identity measured her self-worth by this image. Her husband did not share the same vision, which angered her. As she watched more and more of her friends live her dream, she felt she did not measure up and was a failure. This lit up her core wounding of inadequacy.

The triggered emotion is about us even when the person triggering us is acting inappropriately

The person triggering us is merely the catalyst, not the cause, of our reaction. Without an emotional wound to connect to, we would not have been triggered. However, we might still have been mistreated. In this case, two things are happening at once: we have accessed old wounding—and somebody is mistreating us. There is no reason to overlook that somebody is out of line. We have two separate issues to be dealt with separately.

Jack

Jack, who normally was a loving husband and father, came home from work in a foul mood. As soon as he walked through the door, he yelled at his son for leaving his bike in the driveway. Jack went into the kitchen, saw that dinner was not ready and screamed at his wife Leah, calling her names. Leah was so shocked she started to cry. When he continued to scream, she ran to the bedroom and found herself crouching in a corner, trembling.

It is unequivocally true that Jack's behavior was abusive and inappropriate. Yet Jack was still the catalyst rather than the cause of Leah's triggered reaction. Leah's parents were both physically abusive and Jack's behavior activated the energy of this core wounding.

At the same time, Jack was hurtful and his mistreatment of the family needed to be addressed. This was definitely an issue, but a separate issue from Leah's core wound.

Most triggers are generated by innocent behavior

Though we may be triggered by cruelty or other improper behavior, most behavior that triggers us is innocent. We previously saw the example where Bracken was severely triggered by discussions with Faye about buying a house. It was impossible for Faye to have any clue that when she talked about buying a house she was lighting up emotional wounds from his childhood. In many cases the person doing the triggering does not (and often cannot) know that his or her actions or words will touch on somebody else's old wounding.

The strongest triggered reactions offer us the greatest healing opportunities

Obviously, there are triggers and there are triggers. There is a spectrum of triggers in terms of the energetic charge we experience. Many triggers do not have enough of a charge to be useful in terms of healing. The triggers that give us the biggest jolt offer us the greatest healing opportunities.

Janet

Janet found out that her daughter Annie's boyfriend had thrown Annie's clothes out the window because he thought they were too revealing. When Janet heard this, her body went rigid as a board with rage. Janet's parents had completely controlled her life, down to not letting her see friends after school. She also had felt powerless when her father had moved out because she could not stop it. The massiveness of her triggered reaction helped Janet access her core wounding surrounding feeling impotent.

CHAPTER 14

TRIGGERS
AND THE LAWS OF ATTRACTION

We attract whatever will help us heal

People

As we saw in Part I, by the time we have reached the age of seven all the painful experiences that led us to believe we are unlovable and not enough are lodged energetically in our body. This energy then acts like a magnet that attracts people who light up this energy. The people in our life are not a coincidence. Though we may not realize it at the time, we have attracted into our life our lover, boss, co-workers, neighbors, friends, sales people, landlords, teachers—everybody.

Events

The energy of our unfelt emotions acts as a magnet for more than just people. This energy draws to us people <u>and</u> situations that will trigger us. We attract whatever is needed to unwind the energy of our emotional wounding. This is how we create our lives.

Hank

Remember Hank, who had his first kiss at a party. When he was three, his mother was carrying him and accidentally tripped. He flew out of her arms and hit his head against the coffee table. The physical pain was tremendous and he started to wail. At the same time, Hank unconsciously concluded that his mother had intentionally hurt him, she had rejected and betrayed him, he couldn't trust her and he must be unloved. Because his physical pain was so great, he was unable to feel his emotional pain and it lodged in his body.

The energy of these unfelt emotions became a magnet that attracted events and people that would reproduce the feelings and beliefs of the original incident. Each such situation was an opportunity to unravel the energy of his core wounding.

As we saw, at thirteen he had his first kiss with Laurie and she told him in front of others that he did not know how to kiss. Hank felt profoundly rejected and that Laurie had intentionally hurt him. This incident also reinforced his unconscious belief that he was unloved and women could not be trusted.

In his twenties, Hank took a job where his boss was volatile and capricious. After a good start, the boss publicly announced that Hank was in line for a promotion. Within a week, however, the boss gave the position to somebody else, leaving Hank to feel the world was unsafe and people intentionally humiliated him. Once again he felt rejected, betrayed and that he couldn't trust anyone.

In his thirties, Hank's wife had an affair with a good friend of his. Hank was in total despair that the woman he loved most of all had intentionally humiliated, abandoned, betrayed, rejected and discarded him, which cemented his belief that he could not trust anyone.

With each example, Hank attracted people and situations that lit up the energy of his core wound. Because he was unaware of the dynamics of emotional energy, however, instead of feeling his triggered pain he remained a victim by blaming "life" and other people. Rather than realizing these events were healing opportunities, he viewed them as disasters. As a result, Hank continued to attract people and situations that would recreate the feelings of his old wounding until he understood what he was really doing. His wife having an affair took him into such deep pain that he sought help. He began to feel this pain and his healing journey began.

The laws of romantic attraction

The greatest healing opportunity is in intimate relationships. When we are intimate with somebody, we come up against all our wounding. Whatever is not love surfaces.

Our attraction indicates we have found the perfect person to bring up our baggage

While most people believe the laws of attraction are related to looks, money, intelligence, humor and other traits, these characteristics do not account for the strong energetic charge we feel when we are attracted to somebody. Rather, this energetic charge is the alluring message that we have found the perfect person to light up our wounding.

Emotional healing leads us to the higher purpose of relationships: liberation

This means that relationships are a golden opportunity to heal our emotional wounds and reconnect to our love. Our partner can support our healing and we can support our partner's healing. From a spiritual perspective, the higher purpose of a relationship is liberation and we get there through feeling our emotions.

Mistaking our wounding for love

Because our feeling of attraction is a result of our emotional wounding, we sometimes mistake the emotions of our wounding for love. The truth is the exact opposite: our wounding is the barrier to our love.

For example, when we feel abandonment, rejection or betrayal we are feeling loss, not love. When we feel jealousy we are feeling our insecurity or insignificance, not love. The energetic charge that we experience is about our wounding—we have been triggered and our wounding has been lit up. Rather than feeling love, we are feeling a gateway to our painful suppressed emotions.

The energy dance

Every relationship is an energetic dance. Our energies are always feeling out our partner's, and we react to our partner's energy. This dance will usually recreate the energy dance of our childhood so that we can relive the emotions of our past in order to unwind them. We have picked our partner because of the specific energy dance he or she can provide that will trigger us.

Energy dances can take innumerable forms. A common dance has a contraction-expansion rhythm. This dance may begin with our shutting down, which causes our energy to contract. The more our energy contracts, the larger our partner's energy will expand in order to find ours. Our partner usually becomes frustrated or angry at not being able to feel our energy and having to search for it.

Karen and Tom

Karen grew up with an abusive father and needed to feel her suppressed feelings of powerlessness so that she could access the pain of how dad broke her heart. Karen's husband, Tom, grew up with a downtrodden mother and he needed to feel his repressed anger and resentment towards her for never protecting him.

Tom's energy scared Karen. She was meek around him and her energy would shrink. The meeker she became, the larger Tom's energy would become as his energy sought to find hers. This game of energy hide-and-seek often caused Tom to become overbearing and aggressive. Their energy dance gave each what they needed to be triggered: Karen was able to access her feelings of powerlessness and Tom was able to access his anger.

Gene and Rose

Gene's father abandoned the family when he was five and Gene suppressed his terror at losing his father. Rose's father browbeat and undermined her as a child and she experienced a total loss of self. The energy dance in their relationship was that Gene would maintain a thick wall around his heart while Rose's energy would desperately try to penetrate the wall only to bounce off. With this dance, Rose was able to access her feelings of worthlessness. She finally broke up with Gene and the dance changed. When she withdrew her energy, his energy desperately chased after hers and he tried to win her back. This new dance enabled Gene to access his terror of abandonment.

Why we keep attracting similar partners

We attract people into our life who will trigger painful emotions until we clear them. Without an awareness of triggers, we will not recognize we are being triggered. Instead, we will usually blame our partner for our pain. As we repeat this pattern eventually the relationship might collapse. If we fail to clear the energy of our wounding, we will then attract somebody else who will trigger us in a similar way. This pattern won't stop until we recognize it and take action.

If we realize we have a pattern of attracting people who cause us pain, we may become harsh with ourselves and conclude that we are stupid or self-destructive. What is really happening, however, is that we are unconsciously creating situations where we can heal—but lack conscious awareness of what we are doing.

John

John grew up with a narcissistic father. It was dangerous for him to express himself because his father would become angry and degrading, which caused John considerable pain. John's core wounds were feeling unsafe, insignificant and unloved.

I asked John to do the following exercise: write down all his major relationships and list why each relationship had ended. Towards the end of the exercise, he stopped writing and began to laugh. With the exception of one relationship, he was writing the same thing over and over again.

John continually attracted self-centered women who had a sweet exterior, but were angry and abusive with him. John was attracting, and was attracted to, women who would trigger his core wounding. These girlfriends presented John with the opportunity to tap into his unfelt emotions of resentment, helplessness, sadness and shame.

With each relationship John was unaware that his painful triggered emotions provided him with an opportunity to heal. John would blame his pain on his girlfriends. They were mean, they were bitches, blah, blah, blah. Without awareness of the value of these women to his healing process, each relationship would fail. John then would be attracted to yet another woman who would ultimately mistreat him.

John remained stuck in this loop until he became aware of Core Emotional Clearing. Once he began to clear out the energy of his emotional wounds he was no longer attracted to the same type of woman.

Mutuality: the laws of attraction apply to both partners

In any relationship based on mutual visceral attraction (meaning not based merely on factors of convenience such as money or necessity), the laws of attraction apply to each partner. There is no strong mutual attraction unless both people have core emotional wounds and the other person can trigger those wounds. Though one or both may deny it, there is no "chemistry" where only one person has "issues" and the other has none. Metaphorically, there is only a taut string when there is a pull on both sides.

In the above example, we saw that John's core wounding was feeling unsafe and insignificant. He ended up marrying Candace, who, just like his father, would scream and get angry at him. This would trigger his core wound.

In turn, Candace grew up with a workaholic father who was often absent. At a young age, she personalized her father's absence to mean that he did not care about her and she did not matter. When Candace became aggressive towards John, he would withdraw and become emotionally unavailable. This would trigger Candace's core wound. They were attracted to each other because each triggered the other.

We attract an energetically compatible partner who reflects our level of wounding

We attract partners who match the depth of our emotional wounding. Like attracts like. The more wounded we are, the stronger our attraction to significantly wounded people. Somebody who is open, authentic and connected to love will not be drawn to someone who is closed, inauthentic and disconnected from love.

Who we think to be our soul mate may well be our wound mate: the person who triggers us the most may not be an appropriate lifelong partner. When we become clear, we no longer have the compatibility of wound mates. Our compatibility will depend on how much we enjoy each other. If our only compatibility was our wounding, we may discover we no longer want to be with that partner.

The less emotional wounding we have, the more we are connected to our love and joy. When we live in joy, we attract joyful energy. As a result, Core Emotional Clearing not only improves our emotional health, but also helps us attract an emotionally healthier partner.

CHAPTER 15

THE BIGGEST MISTAKE
WE MAKE WITH TRIGGERS:
EVADING THE TRIGGERED EMOTION

Our pain-avoiding tactics extend to our triggers. The problem is that since triggers are how we access our unfelt emotions, we rob ourselves of a healing opportunity when we avoid feeling them.

Evading a triggered emotion through blaming

The most common reaction to being triggered is to blame the person who triggered us. This is a potent strategy to avoid feeling our pain. When we blame someone, our focus is on the other person. We then do not, and indeed cannot, focus on what we are feeling.

Our tendency to blame can be reinforced by the family dynamics in which we grew up. Some of us may have had parents who fought a lot and frequently blamed each other. That then became our template to blame and make our partner wrong.

Barbara

Barbara was a single mom with two children. She had a low-paying job that she knew was beneath her capability, but she was frozen inside and just couldn't find it in herself to ask for more money. One afternoon her son, Scott, asked if she would buy him a new pair of basketball shoes because he wanted to pick up the sport. She answered: *No, we can't afford them.* Scott then asked his mom: *Why don't you get a better paying job? It would be nice to afford a few things.* Barbara flared up and yelled: *You are so selfish. Why don't you go get a job instead of pressuring me to pay for your shoes.*

Barbara felt guilty, but rather than acknowledge being triggered and feeling the guilt, she took the focus off herself and placed it on Scott. Now Scott was the issue and Barbara got to be angry and hurt, temporarily avoiding feeling deeper feelings of embarrassment and shame. She did not yet have the awareness that here was yet another opportunity to access her wounding in order to resolve her past, which was preventing her from living in abundance.

David

David discovered the family's monthly expenses had skyrocketed. When he showed his wife Fawn the statements, her old painful feelings of incompetence, inadequacy and unworthiness were lit up. Rather than using this as an opportunity, she reacted by screaming at him that he was making her feel bad. By blaming David—thereby avoiding feeling the triggered emotion—Fawn ensured that she would not have to face her wounding.

Bill

Similarly, we saw earlier how Bill became belligerent when accused of flirting inappropriately. With all of his attention devoted to attacking his accuser, Bill avoided feeling his trigger. He was going to defend himself to the death rather than let himself feel the old shame that his sexuality was bad.

Evading a triggered emotion through numbing

Another effective way to evade our triggers is to numb our emotions. By going numb, we avoid feeling pain. For example, Stewart's father frequently belittled him. In order to avoid his anguish, he shut down his emotions. Whenever he began to feel emotional pain, he would automatically flip on an emotional circuit-breaker and go numb.

A more subtle technique is to become tired. We tend not to recognize this as a way to avoid our uncomfortable feelings. For example, during a workshop Gary felt a woman he liked was avoiding him. He became extremely tired and sleepy. When he lay down for a nap, he suddenly got it! He was using his fatigue to avoid his deep feelings of rejection.

Yet another numbing method is the abuse of drugs and alcohol. While genetic factors can be involved, many people who abuse drugs and alcohol have experienced serious trauma that they are desperate to avoid feeling. As the energy of these emotions lives within them, this energy is still there when the numbing wears off. The result is a continual struggle to avoid the pain, which leads to the continued ingestion of alcohol or drugs.

Avoiding triggered emotions can take seemingly different forms

Lana called Nick "chubby," which triggered horrible feelings of inadequacy in Nick. He clammed up for several days and told her he needed time to sort through his feelings. But what really happened was that he had switched them off because he found them too threatening.

Lana then lashed out at Nick. She later said that Nick's withdrawal had pissed her off and she was merely letting off steam so that she could get her anger "out of her system." What really happened was that she had diverted her attention away from her lit-up feelings of insignificance and loneliness, which were the feelings she really needed to "get out of her system."

So while Lana and Nick appeared to be engaging in completely different behaviors—she threw a tantrum and he withdrew—energetically each was doing exactly the same thing: avoiding feeling a painful triggered emotion. They just had different strategies.

Rationalizing our pain avoidance

Lana and Nick each became defensive and felt the need to justify their behavior in order to make their evasion sound constructive. Nick insisted he needed time to sort through his emotions and Lana stressed she was getting her anger out of her system. Rationalizations are often the final piece of our strategy to avoid feeling our triggered emotions.

CHAPTER 16

THE MISUSE OF TRIGGERS NOT ONLY PREVENTS OUR HEALING, BUT ALSO CAN HARM OUR RELATIONSHIPS

Relationships bring up our emotional wounding

How many times have we opened our heart and fallen in love or become infatuated, gotten closer to our partner, become convinced that we have finally met the right person; and then after a honeymoon period we started to fight and we shut down our heart; then we worked through some things, opened up again and recognized how beautiful our partner was; then the next thing we knew the fighting started again, each of us started criticizing the other, our hearts shut down again; and pretty soon we pulled away from each other and didn't want to be in the relationship anymore?

at happened was that our issues surrounding
otional wounding came up. All the aspects of
our self that we do not accept are going to surface in a
relationship. That is why it is so important that we recognize a trigger as being about our emotional wounding. Otherwise, in our agitation and discomfort we
will likely be fooled into thinking that the discomfort
of a trigger is caused by our partner's behavior—in
which case we will blame our partner and not realize
what is really happening.

Misinterpreting triggers can turn healing opportunities into conflict

Blaming our partner can have a serious side effect—it causes separation. Nobody likes to be blamed
and with triggers the blame is not even justified. Our
partner did not cause the painful feeling, but merely
helped spark something that already existed inside us.
Misplaced blame breeds resentment.

To further inflame the situation, when we are triggered our reaction is often greater than the situation
warrants. Not only are we blaming, we are also over-
reacting.

Feeling unfairly treated, our partner often will become defensive and counterattack. This can take the

form of some choice words, including accusing us of being irrational or overly aggressive.

In our pain and anger, we may feel unheard and ignored, and accuse our partner of being insensitive.

Our partner might then become angry, accusing us of being hypocritical and insensitive because of our false accusation.

By this time any opportunities to heal are in the recesses of our rearview mirror. In its place are two upset people who believe they have been mistreated and maybe even betrayed. The situation may even have escalated into anger and yelling, or withdrawal and shutting down. A fight is well underway.

This type of fight starts with a misinterpretation of triggers. The combative drama that unfolds is destructive to any relationship. Every time our partner attacks and blames us, another brick gets laid in the wall of separation. As the wall grows larger, we become more resentful and punishing. Our trust erodes. Our goodwill disappears. Our growing contempt becomes a corrosive presence. There is an avoidance of intimacy: both we and our partner push our energy outwards, and neither will let the other see inside.

So we end up in conflict with our partner instead of healing and getting closer. We either fight or we withdraw. This pattern is highly ironic because we are attracted to somebody to resolve our "issues," yet the surfacing of our issues pulls us apart!

Angela and Patrick

Angela's husband Patrick believed that domestic chores were Angela's responsibility even though she was a working mom. One Saturday afternoon Patrick wanted to watch a football game. Angela complained that she had to do everything and insisted he mow the lawn. This triggered Patrick and he felt a burst of anger. He snapped at Angela that he had worked hard all week and needed a break.

Angela felt a smoldering in her chest and called Patrick lazy.

Patrick now felt even more strongly triggered and responded bitterly to Angela to stop being such a controlling nag.

Feeling attacked, Angela seethed. She reacted by yelling that she couldn't do everything by herself and he should stop being so selfish.

At that moment Patrick just hated Angela. He turned on the game, ignoring her.

She screamed at him that he was childish and good for nothing.

He withdrew even more by having a few beers while he watched the game and continued to ignore her.

She withdrew by becoming silently angry, hating him and vowing never to touch him again.

This episode was another brick in the wall of their separation from each other. Both believed this was more evidence the relationship wasn't working and the other person didn't care. Had Patrick and Angela understood the dynamics of triggers, they would have realized that their reactions were about themselves and not about their partner. They then could have interrupted the cycle of conflict by recognizing they were being triggered. This could have led to their being on the same side and supporting each other's healing.

The continual misinterpretation of triggers can cause a relationship to enter a destructive spiral

Such dramas become more and more corrosive to the relationship with each repetition. In the case of Angela and Patrick, as similar incidents repeated themselves the brick wall became so massive there was no way to save the relationship. They showed less and less of themselves, fearful that their vulnerability would be met by blaming, aggression or judgment. Over time, both felt unseen and misunderstood, and viewed the other as the enemy. They closed their hearts towards each other and increasingly withheld their love, eroding the joy of connection and intimacy they once had.

CHAPTER 17

OUR ATTITUDE TOWARDS TRIGGERS IN RELATIONSHIPS

In relationships we will get triggered

By picking a partner to whom we are viscerally attracted, we are picking somebody who will frequently trigger us. Until we are clear, we are going to have triggered reactions with anyone we are with. By entering into a relationship, whether we are aware of it or not, we have invited our guck to come up. It is important to realize this upfront. Rather than blaming our partner, we should thank our partner for providing us with the opportunity to access the places we need to go in order to heal.

The balance between giving and receiving

Just as we unconsciously chose a partner who can help us access our wounding, so did our partner. When we are conscious of Core Emotional Clearing, we understand that we are in the relationship both for our own healing and also to support our partner's healing. The needs and goals of our partner are as important to us as our own. It is a two way street. We want the same thing: to wake up to who we are.

Being on the same side

When we understand what a trigger really is, we support—rather than judge, belittle, shame or reject—each other. We realize that when our partner is being triggered, it is not about us and we are not to blame. Because we know our partner is hurting, we can be supportive and on the same side rather than defensive. Being triggered is then a completely different experience. When our partner provides us with a safe and supportive environment, we are better able to take risks and feel what we were too afraid to feel before.

Avoiding the trap of mistaking triggers for further "evidence" that we are inadequate or the world is unsafe

Absent an understanding of Core Emotional Clearing, triggers can reinforce the negative beliefs that led to our protecting our heart. We unconsciously create situations that resonate with, and light up, our wounding. For example, Craig's core wound was that his mother was frequently absent and he felt he didn't matter to her. He attracted lovers who were unreliable, which would trigger him. As he failed to recognize these situations as triggers, all he was left with was the pain. He then associated the pain from each new situation as evidence that women were uncaring. Instead of realizing that he was drawing the perfect people and situations to him so that he could access his deep-seated feelings of unworthiness, he reinforced his belief that he was unlovable.

Triggers are the launching point of Core Emotional Clearing

As feeling our unfelt emotions is the key to our emotional healing, and triggers guide us to our unfelt emotions, it is vital to use our triggers properly. Being triggered is the first step in Core Emotional Clearing. We must, therefore, become proficient at this first step in order effectively to launch our Core Emotional Clearing.

SECTION B

THE DYNAMICS OF
CORE EMOTIONAL CLEARING

CHAPTER 18

FUNDAMENTALS OF AWARENESS

We feel our pain to get to our joy

The dark, dense energy of our emotional wounding acts as a physical barrier that blocks us from our light, our real self. In order to clear this energy we need to feel our suppressed pain. The point of feeling our pain is not to glory or wallow in it. Our goal is to unwind the energy of this pain. In the unwinding process we temporarily feel the pain of our wounding more intensely—and then it is permanently gone. We have a more direct connection to our light, which is our authenticity and love. We feel our pain in order to get to our joy on the other side.

We now have the maturity to feel our pain

Through our false identity we have things backwards: feeling our emotions is not the problem, it is the solution. At a young age we begin to create our false identity by blocking our pain because we cannot physically handle it. In order to heal, we need to stop looking at pain from this immature perspective. Now that we are no longer children we have the capacity to feel even the most intense pain.

Keeping our heart open

This leads to the cornerstone awareness:

The mature, and vastly more effective, approach is to keep our heart open and feel all our emotions. When we experience emotional pain, we remain open and completely feel it. The energy of the painful emotion then runs its course and we are free from that emotional energy.

There never is a need to protect our heart, which only leads to emotional wounding. It is by feeling and clearing the energy of our emotional pain that we get closer to our most evolved state, our real self. That's the truth of who we are as human beings.

We have an innate desire to know our self

When we are disconnected from our real self, we are cut off from our essence. Once cut off, we have a strong urge to reconnect with our essence. Our deepest desire is to unconditionally love our self so that we are free to express ourselves fully and share the joy of who we are. We don't feel this desire, however, when our false identity is strong and becomes a cloak.

We create everything in our life

Our life reflects who we believe we are. We create a reality that substantiates our beliefs, whether these beliefs reflect our real self or what we have imagined. When we believe our misperceptions of our self, we create situations that fit these misperceptions.

If we believe there is something wrong with us, we live our life as though there is something wrong with us. If we believe we are unlovable, we create that in our relationships. If we believe we are not enough, then we create situations where we will fail. If we believe the world is cruel, we create situations where we experience cruelty. Our false beliefs cause us to have the bad experiences we fear.

Not only do we protect our heart at an early age, but, absent an understanding of emotional energy, we also subsequently create situations that reinforce our belief that we need to keep our heart shielded. Let's look again at the romantic encounters of Hank, Nancy and George, who had opened up to exploring their sexuality. Each one concluded that their traumatic experiences meant there was something wrong with them. This reinforced their belief that protecting their heart was critical, which drove their partners away. They then become even more determined never to love and trust again.

We have the power to heal

Though we create our life, we tend to draw the opposite conclusion—that we are victims. The truth, however, is that just as we have the power to create our suffering, we also have the power to change. We have the power to open our heart. Our healing is fully within our abilities.

Only we can do our Core Emotional Clearing

Nobody else can do the work for us. Only we possess that power because only we can feel the unfelt emotions of our past. All we need is awareness of the dynamics of Core Emotional Clearing and the willingness to do the work.

Old fairy tales usually have a man saving a woman. Newer fairy tales sometimes have the man and the woman saving each other. These fairy tales, however, are merely symptomatic of how we externalize our internal life. That is what makes them fairy tales. In reality, only we can "save" ourselves. Though we may receive support and guidance from others, there is no way to do the work vicariously. It is our responsibility.

Our desire to be free

Whether we are consciously aware of it or not, we are all instinctively looking to find our way back home. In the deepest recesses of our consciousness we want to live freely. We are all going to the same place and desiring the same thing. While we may be at different stages of the journey, including some who may not yet have left the starting gate, we are all on the same spiritual journey.

CHAPTER 19

THE KEY TO CORE EMOTIONAL CLEARING: SURRENDERING TO OUR EMOTIONS

It is only when we surrender that our emotional energy moves and transmutes

The key to Core Emotional Clearing is not just feeling our emotions, but surrendering to them. It is only when we are in a complete state of feeling that our emotional energy moves. As we continue to surrender, we bring light, which is consciousness, to our wounding. As the light of consciousness touches our dark dense energy, the energy expands and the outer layers become fluffier. While the energy moves, its color changes to the color of the emotion we are feeling. At the same time, as we go through the feelings the density and texture become softer and lighter. The energy unwinds or further expands, loosens and dissipates. At the end of the process, certain layers of our wounding are gone and we have less dark dense energy. Our body is clearer, lighter and more spacious.

What surrender looks like

All our awareness is on what we are feeling

We surrender to our emotions when nothing else exists in our awareness except the emotions—we are not using our mind at all. To put surrendering in perspective, let's look at the spectrum of experiencing emotions.

At one extreme is ignoring and suppressing emotions—we are not even aware of our emotions. This is not surrendering.

Next is feeling with some level of distraction, such as when at the same time we are talking or blaming or playing with the cat. The distraction, whether small or large, is an avoidance of completely feeling our emotions. Instead, we are managing them. We may know there is anger, sadness or fear inside us, but we distract ourselves so that we don't have to feel it all the way. As a result, the energy does not move. This is not surrendering.

Next is intensely feeling the same emotions for extended periods of time. For example, we may cry every night over the loss of a relationship or loved one. Because we are having an intense experience, some of us may wonder why we are not healing. Yes, we are strongly feeling our emotions. But we are not feeling them all the way because we are thinking about the story behind the pain at the same time. This is not surrendering. The emotions' energy will not move.

By analogy, if somebody digs their nails into our forearm, and we don't want to feel the pain, we can take our attention elsewhere. We will still feel the discomfort, just not as fully. If we put our entire attention on our forearm, we will feel all the pain. We can either move away from the pain or towards it.

Healing occurs at the furthest end of the spectrum where our mind is not involved. All we are doing is feeling the emotion. There are no distractions. Our awareness consists solely of the emotion—so much so that we become the emotion. This is surrendering.

Our body remains relaxed

Once we are in a feeling state, we let the feelings take over. No matter how intense or painful the emotions, we relax into them. Rather than tensing our body, we keep it soft. Our muscles are supple. We let our emotions move freely through our body and go with the ride. Just as we are not surrendering when our mind resists by distracting us, we are also not surrendering when our body resists by tensing up.

Imagine being on a roller coaster. We plummet towards the earth and our body is whipped around. Our tendency is to tense up and grip the railing. Even when we put our arms in the air, we are still tense. To take the ride fully, however, means to relax completely while being fully present and aware of everything we are experiencing. We let our body go with the ride rather than resisting it. We give ourselves up to the ride and go with it, wherever it takes us.

The feeling must be authentic

We can only surrender to an authentic feeling. If we are emoting, we are trying to feel something we are not feeling. We are not connected to our emotional energy. Therefore, it will not move. For example, Stella knew she had deep-seated rage, but had difficulty accessing it. She intentionally yelled and shook her body, trying to be angry. Though she was exerting a lot of energy, and appeared to be angry, she was not feeling real anger.

Similarly, Ed was at the beach pounding on the sand with all his might, calling his ex-wife names and screaming profanities. Watching from a distance, I realized Ed was not really feeling and called his name. Ed lifted his head and said *Huh?*—without any emotion whatsoever. Ed had been all sound and movement, but no authentic feeling.

Staying in the now

Though Core Emotional Clearing is about healing emotional wounds that were generated in the past, the work itself is about the present. When we surrender to an emotion, we are focusing on what we are feeling now. When we think of the past or the future, we distract ourselves from what we are feeling now. It is by feeling a triggered emotion in the present that we are able to access the energy of the past.

Detaching from the story behind the emotion

In order to surrender to an emotion we need to separate the emotion from any story behind it. Our healing occurs by surrendering to the emotion, not by recounting the story. Our surrendering is the healing process.

In fact, focusing on the story prevents us from surrendering. As we have seen, the story consists of mind thoughts we generate. It is something we imagine and, therefore, cannot be happening now. What is happening now is the emotion we are feeling.

Memories

When in a deep feeling state, buried memories may surface. They are merely a by-product of Core

Emotional Clearing. We don't need to have memories to have an energetic shift. If memories do come up, it is important not to attach meaning to them. Otherwise, we will be in our mind and no longer surrendering.

Surfacing of an awareness

Sometimes an awareness arises amidst the emotions we are surrendering to. For example, we might have an awareness of aloneness, betrayal or a parent not loving us. There are no stories or images attached to the awareness—it is just a pure awareness. This awareness is not of the mind, but is a deep inner knowing that rises up from our unconscious. The awareness that arise during Core Emotional Clearing do not necessarily represent absolute truth. Indeed, they often reflect our false "truth:" our unconscious negative false conclusions about our self associated with the energy of our emotional wounding. If an awareness does arise, putting our focus on it usually amplifies the emotions we are feeling and we are able to go deeper.

Popping out

While we are surrendering to an emotion we may become distracted by a sound or a mind thought, and pop out of the surrendering. This is not a big deal. Once we have surrendered to an emotion, if we pop out we can always pop back in. We simply put our focus back on the memory of the emotion we just popped out of and the emotion will return. We then surrender once again to the emotion.

Recycling - remaining stuck in the same emotion

Sometimes we keep feeling an emotion and end up wallowing in it. We remain stuck on the surface of the mountain of our wounding rather than breaking through to the layers inside the mountain. Because we are feeling, we may be tempted to believe we are open to our emotions and are processing them. But what's really happening is that part of our focus is on the story instead of solely on our emotions. We remain stuck in the story because we fear what we will feel when we go into the mountain. When we remain stuck in a story, we do not surrender and instead recycle the same emotions over and over again.

Kate

Kate learned that her boyfriend, Scott, had slept with another woman. By surrendering to the shock and horror that rushed through her body, she was able to go to deeper layers and heal. However, if she had instead focused on the story of Scott sleeping with somebody else, rather than surrendering to the emotions she was feeling, she would have remained stuck on the surface and been unable to access the energy of her wounding in the layers below.

Pam

Pam would often erupt into anger at Eddie. This intense anger was a powerful trigger for her to access her emotional wounds. However, she was too afraid to feel the deep sadness and shame underneath this anger and instead would associate her anger with Eddie, blaming him for "making her feel bad." As long as Pam stayed stuck in her anger, she was unable to penetrate the surface and feel the emotional energy of her wounding.

Pam only began to heal when she broke this cycle by surrendering to her anger. Like everybody else, Pam was incapable of surrendering to an emotion and doing anything else at the same time. Such a dual focus is simply outside of human abilities.

In order to do Core Emotional Clearing, there's only one thing we have to do – surrender

Our only action in Core Emotional Clearing is inaction. All we "do" is surrender to whatever emotions come up.

CHAPTER 20

THE BASIC STEPS
OF CORE EMOTIONAL CLEARING

Step 1 - Realizing we are being triggered

We recognize we have been triggered. As we have seen, this is absolutely vital. The red flag is any reaction that makes us feel "lit up." It is that burning sensation, that charge or zing of emotional energy that makes us lash out, attack, blame or defend ourselves.

Using the visual of the mountain of our wounding, this is the surface. We are not yet in the mountain.

Step 2 - Remembering what a trigger is

This step ideally occurs at the same time that we recognize we have been triggered. We need to be aware of the golden rule of triggers, which bears repeating: when we react to a trigger, our reaction is about us and nothing else. Our emotional wounding just got sparked. It is this awareness that enables us to draw our focus inward rather than blaming the outside world for the pain we feel.

Step 3 - Surrendering to the triggered emotion

We surrender to whatever emotion was triggered. As a reminder, no thought or analysis is involved. We don't need to worry about whether we can remember or locate unfelt emotions. We don't need to know in advance where the triggered emotion will lead us. Our emotional body will take care of the path and the details. All we have to do is surrender and let the energy pass through us. Our emotional body will do the rest.

If we do not surrender, we remain on the surface of the mountain of our wounding—and from a healing perspective are nowhere.

Step 4 – Moving from the trigger to the top layer

As we keep surrendering to the initial triggered reaction, the energy of the emotion moves and transmutes. Once this energy has dissipated, the layer beneath the surface becomes accessible and we feel that.

It feels as though the triggered emotion has morphed into the feeling underneath. We are now accessing our unconscious. Drawing upon our visual of the mountain of our wounding, we are in the top layer of the mountain. True healing has begun.

Step 5 - Surrendering to the emotion of the top layer

We treat this next emotion in the exact same manner we treated the triggered emotion. Just as we surrendered to the triggered emotion, we simply continue to surrender, this time to the new emotion. Nothing changes on our part.

Step 6 - Surrendering to any further layers of emotion

It is possible that after surrendering to the top layer this particular Core Emotional Clearing will end. On the other hand, when we are through the first layer yet another layer may be revealed. Indeed, our surrendering may continue to reveal several more layers of our unconscious. We just continue to surrender to each emotion that comes up. It is one continuous ride.

Step 7 - Knowing when we are done with an episode

As we surrender, eventually our emotions subside. There is no next layer and no more feelings come up. The ride stops. We have a feeling of peace and relief.

The key is getting in

The key to taking the ride is the initial surrender. That's what gets us in. Once we are in, there's nothing to do and the choice to surrender is much easier. We just keep going.

The oak tree visualization of our wounding

Our emotional wounding also can be visualized as an oak tree. Our core wounding represents the seed that the entire tree grows from. The seed gets planted that we're not enough just as we are. This grows into our trunk, which becomes the foundation of all of our beliefs. This foundation creates fundamental beliefs that are extremely painful, and sometimes unbearable, such as: *I don't belong here, I am unloved* or *the world is unsafe.*

The limbs of the tree represent our unfelt pain from the misperceptions that grew out of the foundation of our trunk. Examples of these misperceptions include: *I have to hide who I am; I am broken; others won't like me;*

my sexual feelings are bad; I am defective; I am incompetent; I don't deserve love or happiness.

The branches are our inauthentic behaviors that grew from the limbs. These behaviors all contain unresolved emotions that we are still avoiding feeling. Behaviors that grew into branches may include: becoming generous in order to gain acceptance, overachieving, underachieving, not trying, greed, gluttony, prudishness, pornography, rebelling, finding fault with others, feeling guilt or shame, being shy or inhibited, feeling arrogant or superior.

The leaves of the tree are the conscious part of our lives and represent our triggered emotions. They are our reactions to day-to-day events, situations and people. As leaves are whatever lights up the energy of our wounding, they can take any form: we get cut off while driving, somebody walks in line in front of us, our partner comes home late, we can't find our passport, the kids broke a dish, not making the team, getting fired, getting a flat tire, a breakup, unreturned phone calls, bringing a report card home, losing a game, getting a new job—there are infinite possibilities.

Anger is often the triggered emotion

Anger is often the triggered emotion, the leaf of the tree. Anger tends to serve as the emotion that we unconsciously believe "protects" us from feeling the suppressed painful emotions in the layers below— such as sadness, shame, impotence, helplessness, fear, betrayal, abandonment or hopelessness. Put another way, anger lies on top of our pain and is a gateway to the unfelt emotions of our wounding.

All triggers can lead to our core wounding if we are able to keep surrendering

Every leaf of the tree is linked to an inauthentic behavior, which resulted from a misperception of our self and the world, which arose from our fundamental belief that we are unlovable or not enough. It doesn't matter which leaf we "pick"—all leaves ultimately lead to the seed. All we have to do is surrender to the feelings of any leaf and, if we continue to surrender, it will take us to a branch, then to a limb and ultimately down the trunk and to the seed.

We don't need to feel all our wounding in order to heal

The good news is that to heal we don't need to feel every unfelt emotion of our entire life. For example, when we unravel the suppressed emotions of a limb, we unravel all the branches and leaves associated with that limb. This means that to clear our wounding we don't need to feel all the leaves and all the branches of the tree.

Similarly, if we make it all the way to the seed, and completely unwind its energy, we unwind the energy of the entire tree—we clear all of our wounding. The barrier to our essence is completely removed. We are our authentic self. This is the ultimate healing.

Though our core wounding is from long ago, the events of our life today are the way to get there. Triggers are the portals to use the present to heal the past. Our everyday life is constantly providing us with opportunities to access the energy of our wounding. We always have a way in.

CHAPTER 21

CORE EMOTIONAL CLEARING
– INSIDE A RELATIONSHIP

The benefit of being witnessed

When our partner is supportive and encouraging, we can delve more deeply into our emotional wounding. While having a reaction we may feel afraid because we're not sure where it's going to lead—yet with our partner right there with us we're going to feel more supported. We can explore and face a lot more.

Any time we really expose our self, our partner's heart normally opens. There is an intimacy in letting others see inside us. It is the deepest level of sharing. Being witnessed creates deeper understanding, compassion and bonding.

Being witnessed in our pain and vulnerability heightens healing. When we are hurting, it is easy to hide and feel our pain in solitude, free from the judgment of others. Our pain reminds us that we are unlovable and we become vulnerable. To allow somebody to see us when we are vulnerable subjects us to the risk of being rejected, judged, ridiculed or shamed. Being witnessed can be threatening.

When we allow others to see our vulnerability, we are true to our self regardless of their reactions. Instead of hiding who we are, we are exposing who we are. We discover that our fears of being seen were unfounded. We break free of the constraints we imposed on ourselves. Being witnessed heightens our self-acceptance. We have dissolved a part of our false identity that held onto the belief that we have to act inauthentically in order to be accepted or loved. So our energetic shift is more profound and we experience a greater healing.

Our role when our partner is triggered – holding space

Recognizing our partner is triggered

Ideally our partner does not need to stop and let us know when he or she is triggered, and our task is to recognize the triggered reaction. Obviously, we will not feel the burst of energy our partner is experiencing. However, the signs will usually be clear: an abrupt reaction in the form of anger, defensiveness, blaming, resentment or sadness.

Realizing our partner's reaction is not about us

It is important to realize that any reaction is about our partner's wounding and not about us. We do our best not to take our partner's reaction personally. We have nothing to defend against and do not need to become combative. In this way our focus can remain on our partner, where it belongs.

Acknowledging the trigger

If our partner does not recognize the trigger, we can ask a question or make a suggestion: *Ah, you're having a reaction*, or, *can you feel you're having a reaction?* This will remind our partner, who may be overwhelmed, about what is really happening. This suggestion is not a criticism, but rather an inquiry as to whether there's an opportunity for healing.

If our partner acknowledges being triggered, it is important to respond. *I see that. I get that you're triggered.* Then our partner feels supported. If our partner shares with us and does not receive a response, we risk that our partner will feel unheard and alone.

If we notice our partner is becoming distracted, we can invite our partner to stay with the feeling. The basic goal is to support our partner in feeling whatever emotions are arising and encourage our partner to stay with them. It doesn't mean that we need to act as healer or therapist. We are simply there to witness and support our partner by holding a safe space.

Appropriate and inappropriate comforting

Inappropriate comforting occurs when we try to fix the situation by attempting to stop our partner from feeling. We might say: *Don't cry. Everything's OK. It's not that bad.* We are trying to make our partner feel better. This often occurs because <u>we</u> are uncomfortable with our partner's emotions. When we provide inappropriate comfort our partner may temporarily feel better, but no real and lasting change will have been effected.

Providing safe space involves providing our partner with the atmosphere most conducive to being able to feel whatever emotions come up—and not distracting our partner from this experience. Appropriate comforting takes the form of staying present so that we can witness what our partner is feeling and encourage our partner to feel whatever emotions are surfacing.

In terms of touching, we don't touch our partner to make him or her feel better. But touching our partner can be quite effective when we sense our partner needs support and we do not interfere with our partner's experience. In this circumstance, touch (sometimes an embrace) can be highly effective in terms of helping our partner feel supported so that he or she can further let go and drop more deeply into the experience.

When we react to our partner's reaction

Sometimes we will be triggered by our partner's reaction. We can try to put our own reaction to the side. If we are unsuccessful, however, we are not in a position to hold the space for our partner and it is best to go to separate corners.

When things go awry

Even when we want the same thing and make the commitment to be on the same side, there will be times when we fall into our old patterns of hiding, blaming or taking things personally. Our body locks up when we think of sharing our feelings. Telling the truth is not always easy.

When tensions escalate it is time to take a break and be alone to gain perspective. If we remain open and honest, later when we are away from the heat of the reaction we can understand what actually happened. Then we can discuss the experience with our partner from a place of accountability.

An unwilling partner

If our partner is unwilling to do his or her work, or punishes us when we reveal ourselves, that doesn't stop us from doing our own work. We don't need our partner to be present for us to do our Core Emotional Clearing. We can do the work on our own.

CHAPTER 22

CORE EMOTIONAL CLEARING - WHEN WE ARE SINGLE OR OUR PARTNER IS NOT PRESENT

While doing Core Emotional Clearing with our partner is fertile ground for healing, we do not need to be in a relationship to do it. Or we may be in a relationship, but our partner is not present when we are triggered. Life presents us with limitless opportunities. We can be triggered by strangers, co-workers, relatives or even events where nobody else is present.

Healing with a witness

It is important to understand that the power of being witnessed is just as strong when we are witnessed by somebody other than our partner. Being witnessed is being witnessed. The witness can be a relative, close friend or even a stranger, if appropriate. Also, the steps of Core Emotional Clearing are the same as when we are with a partner.

Ellen

Ellen was a woman in her fifties who throughout her life had never been comfortable being touched. Ellen explored with Paul, a man she trusted, being touched in a nonsexual way. As he gently stroked her arms and face her first reaction was to get away, as was her pattern. She felt uncomfortable and scared. Paul supported her and reminded her to be in the moment, permitting whatever feelings that came up to just happen.

Ellen started to cry, allowing herself to be vulnerable and scared. She continued to let go and surrender to these feelings. All of a sudden, memories flooded her awareness of a time when her uncle touched her inappropriately and in reaction she had felt shame and humiliation. She remembered how much she had trusted and loved her uncle, and how profoundly betrayed she had felt at his violation. Anger and rage erupted inside her.

Then Ellen felt a profound sadness at the betrayal and found herself curled up and sobbing. Paul continued to gently touch and caress her. Ellen found herself truly feeling her body for the first time since she could remember. She began to enjoy Paul's touch and was able to surrender even more to the pleasurable experience. She realized how much she loved touch and how sensual she really was.

Paul's witnessing of Ellen's pain helped her have a much deeper healing. She risked rejection when she was at her most vulnerable. Her shift was so profound that she subsequently wanted a full relationship for the first time in her life.

Healing without a witness

The healing steps when we are alone are the same as when we are witnessed: we recognize that we have been triggered; we realize our reaction is about us; we draw all of our focus inward and surrender to the triggered emotion; and we continue to surrender to whatever other emotions come up. Indeed, the steps of Core Emotional Clearing are always the same, whether we are witnessed or not.

When triggered around others

There may be times when we are uncomfortable showing our feelings in front of others. For example, we might be at work and it is inappropriate to express our emotional pain in front of our colleagues or boss. We then have several choices: we can forego the opportunity; we can find a way to be alone; or we can wait until we get home. Once we have found a place where we feel safe, we can draw upon the memory of the incident to bring back the triggered reaction.

As an illustration, Sean was in his apartment talking to some friends. He had a reaction to a friend's story about her father, and felt a strong burst of sorrow. Recognizing that he had been triggered, he got up and went to the next room, where he had privacy. He lay on the floor, closed his eyes and surrendered to his sorrow.

When triggered by ourselves

The work is no different when we are by ourselves. For example, remember Marty who was enraged when another driver cut him off. Marty parked at the side of the road and closed his eyes. As he sat with himself, he felt an electric surge of anger tinged with fear and adrenaline. He surrendered to these feelings and stayed present. He was on the ride and continued to surrender.

Induced triggering

If we don't think that life brings us enough triggers, we can always take classes or workshops where we feel challenged. For example, we can take a dance or voice class where we feel exposed and inadequate. Similarly, we might take a tantra or other personal development workshop where we come face to face with our insecurities.

Risks to doing the work on our own

Some people wonder whether there are risks to doing the work alone. It may feel dangerous because our false identity is dissolving. But feeling is not dangerous. We are emotional beings and feel emotions throughout our entire lives. It is suppressing our emotions that is dangerous and can even lead to illness or disease.

Nevertheless, it is possible that a traumatic emotion may surface while doing the work. Sometimes we may be able to continue to surrender to the intense feelings these memories evoke. And sometimes not—then we can always stop. If these feelings are too disturbing and we are unable to face them, it is advisable to consult a professional healer.

CHAPTER 23

RESISTANCE: THE ROADBLOCK TO CORE EMOTIONAL CLEARING

What is resistance

Resistance is whatever techniques we unconsciously developed to distract us from surrendering to our triggered emotions and the emotions in the layers below. Core Emotional Clearing is simple: all we have to do is surrender. This does not mean, however, that Core Emotional Clearing is easy. We have developed lifelong strategies, which have become patterns, designed to help us avoid feeling uncomfortable or painful emotions.

Why we resist

Our false identity

Feeling pain is precisely what our false identity is "protecting" us from. As long as we continue to misperceive that our false identity is who we really are, we will continue to believe that we are unable to cope with our painful emotions and need to be protected from them.

Because we believe our false identity is who we are, dissolving any part of it feels like we are getting rid of a part of ourselves. As a result, Core Emotional Clearing can be frightening. This is why many people are reluctant to do their healing work. The scariest thing we'll ever do is face our emotional wounding, which consists of the painful feelings associated with our false core beliefs that we are not enough as we are, we don't belong, we are unloved and the world is unsafe.

Though we may sometimes feel apprehensive or scared, dissolving our false identity means its death, not ours.

Although we may fear that in doing Core Emotional Clearing we might not make it back from feeling our despair or grief, the opposite is true. When a part of our false identity dissolves, more of our real self emerges. We experience a rebirth of who we are. The irony of resistance is that the very thing we fear actually liberates us.

Fear of who we are without our false identity

Many of us unconsciously fear we won't know who we are without our false identity. Others may fear there will be nothing to replace it. As a result, we can be scared to let go of our false identity. Let's remember John, whose father was abusive and volatile. Over time, he completely hid (from himself as well as others) who he was in an effort to be safe. He grew more and more disconnected until he completely lost himself. He clung desperately to his false identity because unconsciously he was terrified he would be nothing without it.

Extreme fear

For some, our fears can become so great that we hide and sit on the sidelines of life. We fear even being triggered. We do not want to put ourselves in a position where we might risk rejection and light up emotions we still believe to be unbearable. We see this in people who, despite what they might say, don't want to enter into a relationship or even date. Similarly, remember Paul who went to a party. Though he wasn't conscious of it, his greatest fear was that old feelings of inadequacy and humiliation might be triggered.

Consequently, he remained in the corner and left early in order to avoid any possibility of having to feel his pain.

Perverse pleasure in our suffering

At some level, many of us derive pleasure from our emotional pain. At the root of our false identity is the core belief that we are unworthy, unlovable and not enough. With these beliefs we have a tendency to sabotage our happiness. Not only do we believe we don't deserve to feel good, we also believe we deserve to feel bad. This leads to a perverse pleasure in our suffering.

There are other reasons for this perverse pleasure. As an unconscious strategy, some of us create thoughts over and over again so that we feel sad, angry or victimized. While these feelings may be painful, we know that they are manageable—and they distract us from feeling the deeper unknown pain of the wounding lodged in our unconscious. Because this tactic spared us from greater pain, we kept using it. It became a pattern. It became familiar so it felt safe and comfortable. We found pleasure in it, even though it hurt.

For example, remember Connie. She would spin stories about miserable experiences with her father or about her boyfriend leaving her. Creating familiar and manageable suffering served as an unconscious diversion that "saved" her from facing her deepest pain. As a result, she felt a perverse pleasure in her suffering. She became totally attached to the familiar pain she knew and could cope with.

We can also feel pleasure in our pain when we have a skewed template of love. As we have seen, when we are young we associate with love whatever attention we get from our parents. So if we are frequently mistreated, we falsely associate the pain with love. The pain also becomes familiar and comforting. As a result, at some level we take pleasure in this pain.

How we resist

Once we have unconsciously concluded that it is not safe to be who we are, our behaviors are geared to resist feeling who we fear we are. This is why we developed our false identity, which over time becomes bigger and stronger until we begin the dismantling journey. Here are some of the types of resistance we can face when doing Core Emotional Clearing:

Predominant pattern

When we were children, we developed a favorite defense mechanism to survive unbearable emotional pain. The predominant pattern we adopted depended on our personality. For some of us it took the form of becoming aggressive, controlling or angry. For others, we would withdraw, play the victim or make ourselves really busy. There are also those of us who go numb, or spin stories or become highly analytical in order to keep us locked in our mind. These are all different ways of "checking out" to avoid feeling the pain of our wounding.

As a child, after we unconsciously realized a diversionary behavior "worked" we kept using it. Once in place it was like a habit. It became our default pattern to avoid uncomfortable feelings, especially when we were triggered. If we suddenly feel unsafe, our predominant pattern can abruptly surface. When we are in this pattern, it can occupy our entire awareness, making it difficult to get out of the resistance.

Focusing on the external

As long as we can keep the focus off of us and never allow ourselves to be vulnerable, then we are not going to risk being hurt. Focusing on something happening outside of us can take any form, such as turning on the TV, gossiping, finding fault with the world, blaming others. These all distract us from our pain.

The thought treadmill

Another popular resistance strategy is using our mind to generate thoughts. These thoughts may be very direct distractions such as: *I don't want to feel this* or *I can't do it, it's too much.* Or the thoughts may not specifically be about Core Emotional Clearing—any thought will act as resistance. Our mind is prone to inventing stories, which are products of our imagination and distract us from what is actually happening in the present, including what we are feeling. The more we are disconnected from our self, the more our mind keeps us on a treadmill of thoughts.

Fearful thoughts

As we saw in the chapter on how we create fear, our distracting thoughts can also take the form of stories that perpetuate fear to occupy our attention. The fear is not related to a real danger because the event we fear is something that exists only in the story our mind has created and, therefore, the "danger" is imaginary. This fear dominates our attention because it is our nature to devote our focus to getting away from any perceived danger.

Exerting our will on the outcome of our healing

If we become attached to a certain outcome while doing Core Emotional Clearing—say we want to experience a certain emotion or revisit a certain memory—then we will exert our will on the healing process in order to achieve that goal. Exerting our will, however, fixes us with a certain outlook. It also means we are trying to perform. This robs us of the freedom to feel exactly what we are feeling and have an authentic experience. Our will, therefore, distracts us from surrendering to our emotions and acts as another form of resistance. It also demonstrates a lack of acceptance of our self.

Wanting to be "more"

Sometimes we want to be ahead of ourselves. For example, we might want to project that we live the consciousness teachings, whereas we might currently just understand the teachings though we can't live them yet. We might want to be more evolved, more spiritual or more healed than we currently are. As a result, we are not present and authentic. We are not telling the truth of who we are at the moment.

What to do when we feel resistance

Identifying our predominant pattern

It is extremely helpful to identify our default pattern of resistance. When we are in our pattern, we are blind to it. It is like being in a hole that we are unable to see out of: all we are aware of is the hole. In dealing with this resistance, awareness is the first step. Once we realize that we tend to go to this pattern, we are empowered to observe ourselves in the pattern. We realize it is just our default behavioral pattern. It is behavioral clothing rather than who we are. As mature adults we don't want to wear the clothing of our childhood and can choose to wear different clothing. Awareness gives us choice.

Gaining awareness and observing ourselves spinning stories

When our mind spins a story, we can gain awareness of what is happening and realize that the story is just a mirage. As soon as we realize we are spinning a story, we make the conscious choice to stop immediately. Sometimes we may still have a desire to continue with the story. Stop anyway and let it go. In time, we catch ourselves at the beginning of the story. Eventually, we stop spinning stories.

Remember Joe, who had made a mistake when he inspected a client's home. Joe woke up at three in the morning and could not get back to sleep. His mind kept spinning over and over the same story about how he had messed up: he couldn't get things right. Once in a while Joe would pop out of the story and realize it was just a story. As he witnessed his mind spinning the same story over and over, he finally had a moment of clarity: he was not the story. The story then stopped and he was able to go back to sleep.

Remember also Shari, who broke up with her boyfriend, Mike. Shari kept imagining Mike's parents criticizing her, which kept her in a continual state of anxiety. Shari was so used to spinning stories in her mind that it took her a long time to realize that was what she was doing. Once she had this awareness, however, every time she noticed her mind was spinning one of these stories she would tell herself: *that's a mirage.* The more Shari performed this exercise, the more adept she became at identifying a story as a mirage as soon as it started. These stories then became less and less frequent, and finally stopped.

Embracing our resistance

If we really embrace our resistance, it can act as a gateway to the emotion we are trying to evade. If we experience resistance, have it. Really have it. Resist all the way. Have the *no, I don't want to feel this*. Be with whatever is happening inside. The more we can be with our resistance without judging it, the more it will begin to shift and we will connect with the emotion we are resisting feeling.

Janet

Janet was cooking dinner. When her husband Marty came home from work he said: *oh, we're having spaghetti again.* That triggered anger in Janet, but she didn't want to feel it. The resistance was so strong she felt paralyzed. Marty knew Janet was triggered and it was touching something very deep inside her. He didn't take it personally and encouraged her to feel.

Janet let herself have the resistance and it took the form of saying: *No, I don't want to feel this. No, no, no.* In having her no, Janet's feeling gateways opened and she threw the soup ladle down. She yelled: *I hate you. I hate my life. I hate being a mother. I hate being a wife. I don't want to be here anymore.* Now she was completely feeling her authentic anger. She was in and her ride had begun.

Using voice and movement

When we give voice to what we are feeling, energy moves. It opens the channels to the emotions that we are feeling, but resisting. Using our voice means making a sound or saying words that reflect what we are feeling. Similarly, moving our body also moves energy. We can walk around, run, lie down and throw a tantrum—any movement that amplifies the feeling will be helpful. Using voice or movement will be helpful, but using both at the same time is far more effective.

The hair of truth

Sometimes, despite our best intentions, we are triggered yet still insist on making the trigger about the outside world. We become defensive, avoiding facing our buried emotions. One of the reasons we can become defensive is we don't want others to see us as inadequate or defective. The "hair of truth" is a strategy for this situation when we refuse to acknowledge that we are triggered and become defensive instead. As we lack awareness of the trigger, this strategy requires another person.

The hair of truth involves acknowledging whether there is any truth, even if it's just a hair of truth, to what triggered us. When we acknowledge truth in what we are defending against, we tend to stop defending against it. Having dismantled our defensiveness, we stop projecting our attention outwards. We are then in a much better position to direct our attention inwards and finally acknowledge our triggered reaction.

Paul and Sara

During a discussion Sara told Paul that he was being arrogant. Paul suddenly became angry: *How can you say that! I'm always respectful!* When Sara said he had just been condescending, Paul heatedly disputed it. Sara then asked: *Can you feel a hair of truth that you were being arrogant?* This stopped Paul in his tracks; he could feel that there was *some* truth. He then stopped fighting what Sara had said. As his defensiveness disappeared, his awareness was liberated. He was able to acknowledge his reaction—and he was into Step One of his Core Emotional Clearing.

Rhonda and Jim

On a ski trip where people who had done Core Emotional Clearing workshops together were sharing a cabin, Rhonda looked in the refrigerator for her lunch. She was very hungry after skiing all morning. And her lunch was gone. She became really pissed off and yelled at Jim, who she was sure had taken it: *You stole my lunch!* He started to answer, but she cut him off: *You had no right to take it!* He said: *I thought you were eating at the lodge.* She replied: *How dare you!* He asked: *Are you triggered?* She thundered: *Don't change the subject! You think you're so spiritual, but you're just a thief!*

Jim asked: *Can you feel a hair of truth that you're having a reaction?* Rhonda opened her mouth to yell at Jim that he was deflecting when she admitted to herself that there was a hair of truth. Though still upset with Jim, she realized that her triggered reaction was about her old wounding. This was what the work was all about. She was the one who was deflecting. Jim had wronged her, but she would deal with that afterwards. She brought her attention to how the anger felt inside her.

Willingness to feel is essential

It is up to us to want to feel. The emotions are right there, but we need the willingness to feel them. We don't have to like it, we can even hate it, but we have to feel it to heal it. If we don't want to feel, nothing and no one can make us feel. Then all the strategies to get through resistance are to no avail.

Core Emotional Clearing gets easier

Once we have our first emotional clearing, and our life gets better, we become more enthusiastic to continue our healing journey. It is not that the experience becomes less painful; rather, we become keener to reap the benefits. With positive change we viscerally know that feeling our pain is well worth it. The pain we feel is just energy passing through our body.

CHAPTER 24

EFFECTS OF
CORE EMOTIONAL CLEARING

Our energy has changed and we perceive ourselves and the world differently

Amazing things begin to happen as we heal. Our energy has changed and we feel different from within. Though nothing outside of us has changed, our perception and experience of everything has changed. As within, so without. The following are some of the effects that happen organically and automatically after Core Emotional Clearing:

We accept ourselves more

One of the most enjoyable benefits of the work is that our negative self-judgments lessen. When we un-

wind the energy of our wounding, the negative misperceptions about our self associated with this energy
unwind as well. We have fewer thoughts where we
beat ourselves up, such as: *I'm stupid; I messed up; I'm
wrong; I'm a failure; I can't do anything right; I'm bad; I'm
not enough.* We have less self-doubt. A greater natural
self-acceptance occurs. This is a by-product of the shift
in our emotional energy. We naturally treat ourselves
better: we have more compassion, understanding
and patience. Loving ourselves more is a perk of the
work.

We no longer create painful situations that reenact the past

As the energy of our wounding dissipates, we are
changed. With each unwinding of suppressed emotional energy, we no longer attract situations and people that trigger this energy. It's done—the energy is
gone. We are drawn to and attract emotionally healthier people. The "trauma drama" in our life decreases.

We respond rather than react

We are better able to respond to a present situation
as it is, instead of reacting to the past. For example,
Kathy was feverishly working on her thesis when the
phone rang. Previously in this situation, Kathy would

have become upset with the phone as though it had done something wrong. Now that she was clearer, however, she did not feel a charge and addressed the situation by simply turning off the ringer on her phone.

Similarly, Charlie was extremely jealous of his wife, who had a brain tumor. She was afraid to tell him that a male healer had worked on her because Charlie would accuse her of being sexual with him. Charlie did some deep work, starting with feeling his jealousy and then going back to his core wounds of feeling inadequate and unloved. Afterwards, he was able to respond to his wife's illness by recognizing the value of her healing work and encouraging her to continue seeing the healer.

We don't take things personally

When people belittle, shame, reject or physically harm us, we realize they are acting from their own wounding. We no longer take their mistreatment personally. We may not be able to change their behavior, but we are able to take care of ourselves. We are able to recognize, and express, that their behavior is inappropriate and we will not allow it.

Our relationships with others improve

The shift in energy inside us directly affects our relationships with others. Remember Karen, the meek housewife whose energy would shrink when she was with her overbearing husband Tom. He would become angry when she would disappear because he wanted the real Karen. After they divorced they only spoke to make arrangements regarding the children.

Once Karen started doing Core Emotional Clearing, her relationship with Tom changed. Over time they went to family gatherings and social functions together. Eventually, they became friends and could confide in each other. The change was not about anything Tom did. Rather, it was about Karen's internal shifts.

As Karen reconnected with her real self, her energy expanded and took up its own space. She no longer felt threatened by Tom's big energy. Her energy matched his instead of shrinking. Tom became less aggressive as his energy no longer had to hunt for hers and he could readily feel her. These changes occurred naturally, without any discussions about how to improve their relationship.

We gain insight

Truth is often revealed during Core Emotional Clearing and we gain clarity. Sometimes repressed memories surface during the work that help us piece together our life. We are better able to understand our fears, choices, motivations and behaviors.

Remember Sean, who had been triggered while listening to a friend talk about her father and had gone to an empty room. During his surrendering, memories came up of his father leaving the family. Through his perception as an immature boy, Sean had always believed that his father had left because he didn't want to be with him. He realized the truth: his mother had kicked his father out of the house. Sean understood now in the depths of his being that his father's leaving had nothing to do with him. As he unwound the energy of his wounding, he also recognized that his perception of himself as unworthy of love was false.

We are not dependent on our partner to feel love

When we stay connected to our love within, we continue to feel love even if our partner leaves us or stops loving us. Connected to our love, we are in a state of oneness with our self. In order to feel loved, we do not need to know from somebody else that he or she loves us. If our partner stops loving us, we do not feel devoid of love like we do when we are disconnected. We do not stop being who we are. Our love is constant.

Serena believed that she couldn't love a man if he didn't love her. As she was never completely sure of her boyfriends' feelings, she always held back her love. After Serena's boyfriend broke up with her she was devastated. She allowed herself to surrender to feeling her heart break into pieces until the pain finally dissipated.

Serena then found she felt only love. She allowed herself to let it flow. It was sweet and beautiful. It was her own love she was feeling. She also felt love for her ex-boyfriend and it didn't matter whether or not he was gone.

Uncovering our joy

In the depths of our being is love, untainted by emotional pain and our false identity. After Core Emotional Clearing, we have fewer energetic barriers blocking our love. Therefore, we feel more love. When we feel love we automatically feel joy. Love and joy is who we are. It is the thread that connects everybody— we are in the flow of life. This is the greatest gift of all.

CHAPTER 25

THE BIG PICTURE OF CORE EMOTIONAL CLEARING: ACHIEVING OUR PERSONAL FREEDOM

Freedom is such a beloved goal that many consider it an ideal. Freedom is a central theme of most political campaigns. Countries go to war over freedom. Famous political documents such as the United States Constitution and the United Nations' Universal Declaration of Human Rights have freedom as a primary goal.

What people are really talking about in these contexts, however, is not freedom, but rather the right to have freedom. This is an important distinction because the right to freedom merely gives us the opportunity to be free. It does not on its own actually make us free.

s impossible for any society to make us free. No matter how complete our right to freedom, we are not free as long as we believe our false identity is who we are. As long as we are constrained by fear that we ourselves generate, we are not free. As long as our actions are motivated by obtaining the approval of others, we are not free. As long as fears of inadequacy inhibit us from expressing ourselves, we are not free. As long as we believe we are defective and need to hide aspects of who we really are, we are not free. As long as we feel the need to present a false self to the world, thereby leading an inauthentic life, we are not free. As long as we have shut down all or part of our heart, and therefore cannot feel and love fully, we are not free. Through our false identity we are rejecting freedom.

The most any society can give us is the right to be free. In order actually to be free, we ourselves need to take the active step of exercising this right. Only we can make ourselves free. That is what Core Emotional Clearing represents. When we reconnect with our real self and dismantle our false identity, we take that active step. Our healing requires awareness and effort. But the rewards are spectacular: freedom—the real thing.

SECTION C

DOING
CORE EMOTIONAL CLEARING

CHAPTER 26

DOING THE WORK

The following are accounts of people doing their Core Emotional Clearing work. These accounts are provided to demonstrate what it is like to actually do the work so that we have a practical guide for when we do the work ourselves.

For purposes of illustration, the chapter entitled "The basic steps of Core Emotional Clearing" broke the work down into the smallest possible steps, which totaled seven. For purposes of flow and readability, however, we combined some of the steps as follows so that there are now four:

❤ *Step 1 — realizing we are being triggered — includes the step: remembering what a trigger is.*

♥ *Step 3—moving from the trigger to the top layer—*
includes the step: surrendering to the emotion of the top layer.

♥ *Step 4—surrendering to any further layers of emotion—includes the step: knowing when we are done with an episode.*

Bracken

Background

As we saw earlier, Bracken and Faye's discussions about buying a house invariably became volatile and confrontational. Their worst fights came out of these "talks." Bracken always assumed that he reacted so strongly because of financial pressures and because he was intending to switch careers. Faye had declared at the beginning of their marriage that she was going to quit her job and be a stay-at-home wife.

The work

Step 1 - Realizing we are being triggered

One morning Faye told Bracken that she hated living in their apartment and reiterated that she really wanted to buy a house. When Bracken responded that he thought the real estate market was going to go down, Faye started yelling at him. He yelled back, calling her names and accusing her of being manipulative. Suddenly, to his shock, for the first time in decades he burst into tears. He realized something important was happening and sensed his sorrow was about himself, not Faye.

Step 2 - *Surrendering to the triggered emotion*

Feeling disoriented, he sat down. The sadness cut so deep it was a relief to finally express it. His sadness flowed like a strong current; he stayed connected to it and went along for the ride.

Step 3 - *Moving from the trigger to the top layer*

Bracken's sadness became more profound. A memory popped up of when he was twelve years old and his mother would withhold her love if he didn't fight his father (her husband) for her, even though he was scared of his father. Sobs racked his body. The sadness was piercing and the tears kept pouring. His chest was shaking. The sadness and grief felt overwhelming. His head seemed to crumble. He wailed from the depths of his being. The sadness was primal and searing as he let himself feel the unfairness of it all.

Bracken started to analyze the accuracy of the memory and wondered if his mother really was that manipulative. He became aware of the sounds around him and opened his eyes. The ride was over.

Step 4 - Surrendering to any further layers of emotion

There were no further layers.

Comments

Being triggered over buying a house was Bracken's gateway to his unfelt sadness over how unfair life felt. The feelings of unfairness that came up over having to buy a house when he lacked the means led to the much deeper wounding of feeling he had to fight his fearsome father while still a child. As a child, Bracken should have been the protected, not the protector. Though he was already twelve in this memory, this was the layer Bracken hit first. There were many more layers underneath of feeling unprotected that stretched back to infancy.

Though Bracken only went to one layer of his wounding, he still had a profound shift that permanently changed him. He felt more at ease around others and became more gregarious. He had a greater sense of his rights and became more assertive. In his business dealings, instead of lacking leadership he naturally did whatever it took to get the job done, including directing others. Also, discussions with Faye about buying a house lost their charge and he began to explore the idea without reactivity. It was as though it was a different topic.

This was Bracken's first time "in." He did well to surrender to the extent he did. Bracken went as deep as he could at that particular time, and then he came out of the feeling state. Bracken's emotional background was that as a child he intentionally tried not to feel and with practice became a "professional" number who lived in his mind. When the Core Emotional Clearing became too intense for him, he went to a familiar and "safe" place: his mind.

This is normal for anybody who has long practice of pushing down his or her emotions, which is the case for virtually everyone. Bracken was so used to being numb that this was enough for his first go. Not to worry! There will always be plenty of opportunities in the future to go deeper—guaranteed.

For purposes of illustration, the remaining examples are of much deeper experiences by people who have had a lot of practice with Core Emotional Clearing. These more profound experiences help demonstrate the full range of Core Emotional Clearing. Please keep in mind that when we start out our experiences will be more like Bracken's than the following anecdotes. The last example is a Core Emotional Clearing that Bracken did two years later when his ability to surrender was much more developed and he was able to touch his core wounding.

Kathleen

Background

Kathleen had a long-distance relationship with Scott. Over a period of a year they spent approximately six months together, traveling back and forth to visit. Scott wanted Kathleen to move to his city, but Kathleen was unable to because of her work. Scott became friends with another woman, Lisa, with whom he started spending more and more time.

The work

Step 1 - Realizing we are being triggered

One day, Kathleen and Scott were on the phone and Scott told Kathleen that he had slept with Lisa. Kathleen immediately felt shock and horror rush through her body. Kathleen told Scott she felt betrayed and needed to get off the phone.

Step 2 - Surrendering to the triggered emotion

Kathleen dropped down to the floor and sobbed. The thought of Scott and Lisa together was extremely painful. She allowed her grief and pure sadness to move through her. Even though this was physically excruciating, and she was crying uncontrollably, Kathleen surrendered by relaxing her entire body and staying present with her intense anguish. By relaxing her body (instead of tensing and resisting) and by remaining completely connected to what she was feeling, the sensations and feelings moved unimpeded.

Step 3 – Moving from the trigger to the top layer

A feeling of rejection passed through Kathleen. She felt completely unwanted. An awareness arose: she had not been chosen—Scott had chosen somebody else over her. Every time she would connect to this awareness a new wave of grief would pass through her and she continued to sob uncontrollably.

Because of her surrender, memories organically arose. Kathleen began to feel deep-seated emotions of not being chosen by her father, who had abandoned the family for another family when she was four. Now she was in her unconscious. She felt as though her heart literally was breaking in two. She kept surrendering to it, dropping in so profoundly that nothing else existed except the feeling that her heart was breaking. Though the memory helped Kathleen access the energy of this layer of her wounding, once she felt this new energy the memory disappeared and she was in a pure feeling state.

Step 4 - Surrendering to any further layers of emotion

As the energy of not feeling chosen unwound, the next layer was seamlessly revealed. Feelings of abandonment, complete insignificance and being unloved arose. Kathleen continued to surrender to these new emotions, which were close to unbearable. She still felt her heart was breaking. Although it was excruciating, Kathleen continued to remain completely present to everything she was feeling while keeping her body soft by relaxing her muscles.

The feelings came in waves: they would be really intense and then subside until a new wave hit. Occasionally a memory briefly would pop up of a situation with her father. Each memory would reinforce or heighten her feelings of being abandoned and unloved. Kathleen continued to surrender to each emotional wave, whether or not there was a memory attached.

Finally, there was no new wave of emotional pain. Her crying stopped. The ride was over. Kathleen was in a place of quiet. She felt a great sense of relief. Her heart felt lighter and more expansive. Her chest and belly felt less dense and more spacious. She stayed in this experience for some time as her body integrated the repatterning of her emotional energy. Eventually, she felt like standing up and did so, getting on with her day.

Comments

The emotional wound that had been lit up was Kathleen's abandonment by her father. What was happening in the present, Scott's infidelity, was just the trigger. It had never before occurred to Kathleen that these two events were linked. But the triggered emotion automatically led her to the original core wound of abandonment with her father, which was the source of all her reactions surrounding abandonment.

Her father had left the family when Kathleen was four and had moved in with a woman who had three children. Kathleen rarely saw her father after that. She took this to mean that her father had chosen these other children over her. By completely feeling the pain of having her father choose others over her, Kathleen brought consciousness to these old suppressed emotions. As a result, their energy changed color and unwound, becoming lighter and clearer.

After this experience, Kathleen expressed her feelings much more naturally and felt more authentic in her expression. Her previous tendency to feel frozen or self-constrained had shifted. She was less self-conscious and just went about her life. Her mind became quieter as she had less "mind chatter." She was able to be more present when she was with others and really listen to them. Though she had just experienced what is commonly viewed as a romantic disaster, Kathleen felt joyous love. She felt unafraid to love again and, in fact, relatively soon thereafter found a local man with whom she has been very happy.

Marty

Background

Marty had a history of road rage. He took other people's driving mistakes personally. He would become irate, sometimes yelling at or flipping off other drivers.

The work

Step 1 - Realizing we are being triggered

Marty was driving his car when another driver cut him off. This really pissed off Marty. He stopped his car in front of the other vehicle and tore his door open in order to get in the other driver's face. Suddenly, he asked himself: *what are you doing?*

He had an instant awareness that the magnitude of his anger was out of proportion to the situation. This was not about the other driver. Marty became very curious about what was happening inside of himself.

Step 2 - Surrendering to the triggered emotion

He parked at the side of the road and closed his eyes, turning his awareness inside so that he could just feel. He felt an electric surge of anger tinged with fear and adrenaline. He focused solely on these feelings, allowing the energy to move through him. He lost all awareness of his surroundings.

Step 3 – Moving from the trigger to the top layer

After the anger ran its course, Marty felt fear and a sensation of being out of control. As he let himself fully feel the fear, a wave of panic began to arise. His body started to shake and he screamed. Though terrified, he kept all his awareness on his panic and did his best to keep his body relaxed. The waves subsided and then a new wave of panic coursed through him. The panic kept coming in waves.

Step 4 - Surrendering to any further layers of emotion

Though no memories came up, Marty had a knowing that with each wave of panic he was feeling deeper and deeper layers of suppressed feelings surrounding being out of control. He surrendered so completely that the energy of his panic finally unwound and dissipated. The waves then stopped and he felt a profound calmness. He felt lighter and could feel his body more fully.

Comments

Marty's anger covered painful feelings of impotence. This feeling of having no control over his external reality was terrifying. His anger acted as a diversion that would take his attention away from his vulnerability so that he wouldn't have to feel it.

When Marty previously reacted to any perceived slight on the road, his anger would linger for minutes or even hours, while his mind would conduct a running commentary about what a lowlife the other driver was. This time, after the incident Marty no longer felt any anger and there was no ongoing commentary. Marty experienced a major energetic shift and never had road rage again.

Though Marty initially made the triggered emotion, his anger, about somebody else, he was able to adjust. He sensed that if intense feelings were coming up then his attention was being called inside to feel rather than do the usual: make up a story in his mind about how the world was doing something to him. He could clearly see that the conversation his mind wanted to have was to blame and punish the other driver. This was a fight or flight response. As Marty later put it, fighting or fleeing had "the stink of familiarity," with no possibility of producing a healing shift inside of him.

Greg

Background

Greg felt it was impossible to satisfy his father. No matter what he did it was never enough. His father was demeaning and found fault with most everything he did. When Greg was a teenager, he used to get up at 6 a.m. in order to be more productive and please his father. Greg's father, who got up even earlier, would greet him with the sneering question: *Well, what have you done today?*

The work

Step 1 - Realizing we are being triggered

One night over a candlelight dinner at home when Greg was in his thirties, his girlfriend, Iliana, asked him what he got done that day. Greg felt a rush of helplessness and inadequacy. He realized he was triggered and told Iliana, adding that he wanted to focus on what he was feeling. She became angry, feeling he was rejecting her. Greg made the choice to feel what was coming up for him anyway. He got up, saying this was important to him, and went into his office.

Step 2 - Surrendering to the triggered emotion

As he opened the door to the office, he heard Iliana yell after him that he had ruined the dinner she had prepared. He felt pressure and burning in his chest, and tightness in his belly. His feelings of helplessness and inadequacy intensified. His knees buckled and he lay on the ground, surrendering to the feelings swirling inside.

Step 3 – Moving from the trigger to the top layer

As he continued to surrender to his feelings of helplessness, memories of his father's sarcastic tone emerged and he felt resentment. Wave after wave of deep resentment racked his body. He sobbed in despair. Soon he began to dry heave as the energy moved through him.

Step 4 - Surrendering to any further layers of emotion

All of a sudden, hatred and anger raced through his body. He began to scream over and over *I hate you* and pounded the chair cushion. Greg was so connected to his anger that the energy took over. Rather than becoming tired, he was pumped with boundless power and strength.

A deep sadness came up. He lay on the floor and cried as though his heart were breaking. Soon memories came up of his mother promising that he would inherit the house he grew up in—but instead she had willed it to Greg's stepfather, who sold the house without even informing him.

Anger at his mother took over and he raged at her. He yelled obscenities and called her names. Abruptly he felt intense despair and had an awareness of betrayal. He curled up in a fetal position and wept. Every time Greg put his focus on the awareness of betrayal, more tears would come. Waves of emotion went through him, with the waves alternating between anger, impotence, betrayal and abandonment. With the first wave of abandonment, memories arose of his mother and all the men she had put before him. His heart broke and he felt the depths of his despair that he was not enough. He was now feeling his core wound.

Eventually, the pain subsided. There were no more waves of emotion. Greg was spent. He felt a peaceful stillness. His body felt lighter. He felt a great sense of relief and his life made more sense to him.

Comments

The trigger was Greg's girlfriend, which lit up wounding with his father. By continuing to surrender, Greg was able to access much deeper wounding with his mother. We never know where Core Emotional Clearing will lead. But if we completely surrender, the ride will take us where we need to go and show us what we're ready to face.

Through his awareness during and after the work, Greg realized that he had never let himself have his suppressed feelings of hatred and resentment towards his mother. He had felt guilty about having these feelings and had been scared of losing her love.

Greg also realized that throughout his life his mother had been so desperate for love that she would spurn her own son to get or keep a lover. He was angry and felt betrayed because his mother would discard him if she believed he was getting in the way. This was not a reflection on him, rather it was her weakness. Greg knew she did not have it in her to be stronger and he was able to forgive her.

Greg's experience illustrates that the deeper wound is not always with the obvious person. Though Greg's father was consistently belittling, Greg's deeper issues were with his mother.

Towards the end of Greg's Core Emotional Clearing, he went back and forth between feelings of anger, impotence, betrayal and abandonment. Greg would feel the same emotions repeatedly for two reasons. The same emotions were present in different layers. And sometimes he would not feel all of an emotion in a layer and would go back to that layer.

Though Greg touched his core wound of not being enough, he did not go all the way through. As a result, though he unwound some of the energy there was still more to feel. It is very rare to completely clear core wounding all at once. Once we access our core wound, we usually need several visits in order to completely clear it. This can also be true of other layers.

Nevertheless, Greg was profoundly changed. Afterwards, whenever Iliana asked him about his day, it was just a normal question to him without any charge. As he no longer reacted to Iliana as though she was his father, Greg felt much closer to her. He was more playful and laughed freely. His heart opened towards her and he organically did little things to honor her such as bringing her flowers, helping with the dishes and telling her more often he loved her.

Iliana

Background

The plot thickens.

The work

Step 1 - Realizing we are being triggered

After Greg left the table, Iliana was stewing. When she realized he wasn't coming back, she became angry. She picked up the plates to throw the food away—then heard Greg's sobbing. Hearing his pain touched her heart and she started to cry. Iliana felt sorry for Greg, and then realized she was feeling her own sadness.

Step 2 - Surrendering to the triggered emotion

She sat back down with her arms on the table, cradling her head on her arms, and really let the tears flow. Hearing Greg helped her to drop in.

Step 3 – Moving from the trigger to the top layer

Iliana kept weeping. She remembered how much she loved her dad and how much she just wanted her dad growing up, but he was always away working. Memories of waiting for her dad flooded her awareness. She had a deep longing for her father and missed him terribly. She sobbed with a profound grief of longing. In the past she had reached this point, but had held onto the thought of her father. This time, she dropped completely into her sadness with no thoughts or images attached. She was in pure sadness.

Step 4 - Surrendering to any further layers of emotion

An awareness arose from within: daddy doesn't love me. This dropped her. She let go so fully she slid onto the floor. Sobs racked her body. Another awareness arose: I am not enough. She felt her heart was breaking and it felt unbearable. This was why her father didn't love her.

Iliana became engulfed in hopelessness and despair and she totally gave in to these feelings. Waves of despair surged through her body. She felt like she was dying and still she took the ride. The waves just kept coming and were especially intense when she focused on the awareness that she was not enough.

Once she came through to the other side of her despair, she saw herself as a small child in all her purity, innocence and beauty. Iliana wept tears of joy and love. She repeated over and over: *I'm so sorry.*

Soon she experienced a brilliant white light and felt overwhelming love. She felt boundless and ecstatic. Her world felt perfect.

Comments

When we are around somebody else who is surrendering to a feeling, such as Iliana with Greg, it often stirs up our own emotions. We feel a resonant pain. This can make it easier for us to drop in.

Iliana was previously familiar with grief. All her life she had a longing for her father and frequently cried over him. Nothing changed because she was merely recycling the grief she was aware of. She was stuck on the surface until she surrendered to it. Then she was finally able to drop into the wounding underneath: feeling unloved by her father. This led her to her core wound of feeling she was not enough and unlovable.

Though Iliana's father really did love her, an awareness nevertheless arose during her process that he did not. This was a false belief she had carried based on her need for her father and her internalization of his long absences.

As Iliana unwound the energy of her wounding, she also dissolved pieces of her false identity. This is why Iliana felt like she was dying. Something was dying—her false identity.

When Iliana repeated: *I'm so sorry,* she was apologizing to herself for abandoning and rejecting herself as a little girl.

When Iliana experienced a brilliant white light she was reconnecting to her light within, her essence. That's why she felt overwhelming love. The sensation that goes with this is a feeling of tremendous joy, which can feel ecstatic.

Iliana experienced a palpable shift. She used to swim in negative thoughts and feel victimized when something went wrong or she didn't get her way. This lifelong pattern of judging and blaming everyone receded as she began to recognize the pattern. She stopped thinking about how others could get her what she wanted and looked to herself first. She really came into her own and felt liberated. Without thinking about it, she stopped putting herself down and making herself wrong. She talked more freely about her feelings, wants and needs, and was unselfconscious about asking for what she wanted.

This shift also brought Iliana and Greg much closer. There was more ease and patience in the relationship. They were more playful and affectionate with each other. They were more comfortable sharing their hiding places and vulnerability, which deepened their bond.

Samantha

Background

Samantha, who was adept at Core Emotional Clearing, rarely spent more than three weeks at home because she travelled frequently for her work. One time she had a six-week stretch at home and felt bored. A friend, who was also a healer, told her maybe she wasn't bored, she was lonely. Although she didn't feel lonely, Samantha took the healer's words to heart because she trusted him and decided to explore her boredom.

The work

Step 1 - Realizing we are being triggered

She deliberately set the scene to do some inner work and see if she could find loneliness. She built a fire, lit candles, put on some music and sat down on a recliner in front of the fireplace. She brought her focus into the feeling of being bored. As she sat with being bored, the feeling of aloneness permeated her aware-ness. She began to feel what it was like to be alone.

After a while, she felt really alone and it had a quality of sadness.

Step 2 - Surrendering to the triggered emotion

Samantha just let herself feel the sadness. Soon the sadness surrounding her aloneness became painful and she began to cry.

Step 3 – Moving from the trigger to the top layer

Memories came up of extremely happy times with her sister and brother-in-law, and Samantha felt how much she missed those times. The feeling of aloneness intensified and the longing hurt her heart as she realized she had never had that close a connection since. She kept feeling her sadness.

Step 4 - Surrendering to any further layers of emotion

An image of her late father floated into her consciousness and Samantha immediately felt so lonely she longed for him. His image lingered and she went into a deep grief, staying there until it passed. She did not feel waves, but rather a constant grief that she allowed to be there and kept opening to.

Abruptly, Samantha saw spirits and immediately felt she knew them and longed to be reconnected with them. She experienced the heart-wrenching loss of being separated from these spirits who felt like family.

She wept with the deep longing and sadness of missing them.

Suddenly, Samantha knew her loneliness was about being disconnected from the ultimate Father, the Creator. She went into a profound sadness and grief. The feeling of loneliness had the same quality as with her dad and the spirits, except it felt vaster and more intense. She experienced an ultimate feeling of loneliness.

Samantha eventually came though the loneliness and was calm. She sat in front of the fire for a long time, integrating her experience.

Comments

Because Samantha had practiced Core Emotional Clearing for a long time, she was able to "go in" and take the ride quite easily and reach very deep layers.

Samantha's Core Emotional Clearing had a theme: loneliness. It started with her feeling alone, and then went into deeper and deeper layers, until she ultimately felt her separation from the Creator, which was the original source of her loneliness.

Samantha never felt that sense of boredom again. Over the years she spent extensive periods of time alone where she rarely saw another person, yet only occasionally felt lonely. When she did feel lonely, the quality of the loneliness had completely shifted. It was more a sense that it would be fun to have somebody else around rather than the uncomfortable agitation she felt before.

When Samantha looked out at the world it was from a much deeper place within. She felt at peace and grounded in herself. Negative thoughts about the future subsided and many things that used to worry her no longer came up. She was relaxed in her being and more connected to the people in her life. There was a new lightness, joy and openness: she felt alive.

Suzanne

Background

Suzanne was molested by her uncle when she was a child. Throughout her life Suzanne felt anger—anger that she was molested, anger at who did it, anger at all men, anger at the world, anger at herself, anger at her parents. She felt angry most of the time.

Suzanne and her boyfriend, Henry, had taken Core Emotional Clearing classes and had a good understanding of the work. They had numerous discussions about what to do if the other was triggered.

The work

Step 1 - Realizing we are being triggered

One night Suzanne and Henry were playfully wrestling on the bed. At one point, they were rolling together across the bed when Henry pinned her down. Suzanne felt a surge of anger directed at Henry so intense she wanted to hurt him. They had just been laughing and having a great time—Suzanne realized her anger was coming from within and had nothing to do with Henry, who realized Suzanne had been triggered.

Step 2 - Surrendering to the triggered emotion

Suzanne suddenly wanted to hide her anger from Henry because her anger embarrassed her. Henry encouraged her to just let go. She took this opportunity and surrendered to the anger itself, no longer attaching it to Henry. She kept her awareness on how the anger felt in her body. Once she took this critical first step, she was in a pure state of anger.

Step 3 – Moving from the trigger to the top layer

As the anger coursed through her body, she grabbed her lower belly and roared with a primal rage. Because she really let herself have her rage, she moved through it quickly. The transition to the emotion under the anger, overwhelming shame, was immediate. She was now in her unconscious.

Suzanne abruptly bounced off her feelings of shame and went into her mind. Realizing she had "popped out," she brought her focus back to her feelings of shame and surrendered to them again. She felt overwhelmed by an intense humiliation as her stomach and chest felt like they were burning. She started to cry and stayed present to the uncomfortable sensations. Waves of shame, humiliation and uncontrollable crying ran through her body.

Step 4 - Surrendering to any further layers of emotion

Suddenly she felt repulsion and disgust, which produced sensations of nausea. What seemed like endless waves of disgust surged through her body. Eventually, graphic memories surfaced of her uncle forcing his penis into her mouth. She started to heave. (Henry grabbed a towel for her.) As she continued to surrender to the disgust, her body released energy by vomiting. At the same time, she was overwhelmed by feelings of betrayal by her beloved uncle. This was heart-wrenching and sobs racked her body. After feeling numerous waves her body became still. Her crying slowly receded while her chin quivered.

Soon feelings of anger at her mom and dad surfaced: they had not protected her and they weren't there to help her. She began crying in anger. An awareness arose that her parents had no knowledge of her uncle's actions. Waves of feelings of just wanting her mom flooded her. She said: *I want my mom.* Henry moved next to Suzanne and silently held her. Feeling his presence and love—feeling safe—opened the floodgates and she cried like a child, repeating over and over: *I want my mommy.*

Eventually the next layer was revealed and Suzanne felt helplessness. It was a horrible feeling to have no control whatsoever and be at somebody else's mercy. She also felt the searing grief of having her innocence ripped away forever without her consent or control—such a precious part of her she'd never get back. While Henry continued to just hold her, Suzanne's heart felt as though it was breaking into pieces and she cried in deep sorrow.

In time, the waves of helplessness and grief subsided. A sense of peacefulness washed over her. A feeling of clarity and light emerged inside of her and she felt profound love. She felt more spaciousness as though a great weight had been lifted. She touched her body as if feeling herself for the first time. Suzanne kept repeating: *wow, I feel so different.* She felt incredibly light and had a wonderful sense of ease and joy.

Comments

After Suzanne popped out towards the beginning, her Core Emotional Clearing was one continuous ride. Though there may have been lulls, Suzanne was always "in." Because she continued to surrender and stay on the ride, she was able to go into deeper and deeper layers of her unconscious.

To many, it appeared that when Suzanne was angry she was working through her molestation. However, she was stuck in anger. Anger is frequently the emotion that lies on top of our emotional wounds, protecting us from the hurt below that was too overwhelming at the time we first experienced it. This surface emotion was Suzanne's gateway to healing, not the healing itself. She needed to get beneath the surface layer in order to heal.

Having somebody hold us can often help us go deeper in our healing process. When we feel supported and seen, it helps us to open up and relax. We feel safe and our emotional body automatically lets go. It's like magic. It gives us permission to authentically feel.

The person witnessing us does not need to do or say anything. All we need is for the person to be present, connected and supportive. Any conversation or attempts to control the situation will take us out of our feeling state. The witnessing should be supportive of our experience rather than interfering with it.

Suzanne's anger at her parents was not a logical conclusion since her parents were unaware of the event. But that's irrelevant. It was a feeling that came up in her process and she had to let herself feel that. Even if it did not represent absolute truth, it was her truth arising out of her immature perspective as a child. The key is to feel whatever arises without judging it with logic.

In molestation cases, the toughest layer can be feeling robbed of our purity and innocence. Once it is taken from us, it is lost forever.

After this Core Emotional Clearing, forgiveness occurred naturally and organically, without any thought or intention. Suzanne forgave herself for closing down her heart and causing a life of separation, fear and loneliness. She forgave her uncle because she realized that his actions were not about her and she was not the cause of his behavior. She also forgave her parents because she knew they could not prevent the incident.

Suzanne experienced a true unwinding of emotional trauma from her molestation and became free to open her heart and be herself. She felt an inner freedom and her shame was gone. She was in the world without feeling self-conscious. She was more animated and assertive, and took on leadership roles. Rather than being stuck in anger and shame, she was able to embrace her femininity and sexuality. She was transformed: instead of being angry, Suzanne was happy and joyful.

Bracken

Background

This is Bracken from the first example—two years later. Bracken ended up divorcing Faye because he became devoted to his emotional healing, but Faye had no desire to pursue her own healing and dismissed his healing efforts.

He was visiting some friends who were throwing a New Year's party. His friends' living room and kitchen, which were going to be the center of the party, were a mess. He wanted to make the house festive and look good for the party, but did not want to take on the entire project by himself. He asked his friends for help, but they flatly refused.

The work

Step 1 - Realizing we are being triggered

Bracken felt extremely agitated. His head was buzzing and burning, and his chest was swirling. He went for a walk in order to "let off steam." He was halfway down the driveway when he realized he was triggered, and told himself to drop into the feelings behind his discomfort.

Step 2 - Surrendering to the triggered emotion

Suddenly, Bracken doubled over, his hands on his knees, and started sobbing. He told himself to relax into it. A new wave of grief ran through him.

Step 3 – Moving from the trigger to the top layer

Bracken was in his unconscious. It happened very quickly and abruptly, like standing on a trap door and the door falls open.

He had an awareness of always having to "go it alone." Grief passed through Bracken in ebbs and flows. As each wave hit, he cried uncontrollably. The wave would ebb and then the next wave would hit.

Step 4 - Surrendering to any further layers of emotion

When Bracken put his focus on the awareness of his aloneness, his heart would hurt even more intensely with a throbbing pain. The pain became overwhelming, but he reminded himself to keep ease in his body. At one stage he found himself on the ground. The waves of grief kept coming. His sobbing was not very teary; it was more a shaking kind of crying that felt directly connected to his heart.

During a lull, where he thought the Core Emotional Clearing was over, Bracken stood up. He opened his eyes. Seeing the driveway, the trees and the sky was jarring because he had completely lost awareness of anything but his feelings. It was so jarring he immediately closed his eyes. His awareness went back to his "aloneness" and he doubled over as the next wave of grief ran through him. After feeling several more waves of grief, Bracken vomited. Though vomiting normally was difficult for Bracken, it happened very easily.

Afterwards, the waves of grief continued. An awareness of injustice arose from his unconscious, and his despair was so agonizing that he began to wail. His heart hurt so much. He thought it was never going to end, but he continued to surrender anyway.

When the waves stopped and Bracken felt spent and exhausted, he stood up, keeping his eyes closed. A bright, white light appeared. It was beautiful and reassuring, beyond words.

Then another wave of grief hit and Bracken doubled over again. He was sobbing, but at the same time Bracken felt a profound joy. Though his heart hurt intensely, he felt a rejoicing. An awareness arose that he was feeling his heart—he was no longer alone. He had found himself.

Comments

Bracken's experience illustrates that memories don't have to come up. If memories do arise, they are a by-product of the healing process, not a part of it.

While sometimes there are different emotions in each layer, in this case Bracken mainly felt the same emotion in each layer: grief. This was the theme of his Core Emotional Clearing. Bracken had a universal core wound that arose out of feeling separate. Aloneness is separation, and separation causes deep feelings of grief, anguish and heartache that Bracken had continually suppressed throughout his life.

By finally surrendering to a trigger that lit up his core wounding, Bracken was able to feel his grief associated with aloneness. By continuing to surrender no matter how intense the pain, he was able to access deeper and deeper layers of his wounding surrounding separation. This enabled him to unwind the dark pockets of previously suppressed grief and despair that had accumulated over the course of his life.

If Bracken had stopped this Core Emotional Clearing earlier, the work still would have been beneficial. Afterwards, he would have felt lightness and relief. He would have had a significant energetic shift that would have permanently changed him from within. But because Bracken continued to surrender, he was able to go so profoundly deep that he found his joy underneath his pain. This is the ultimate goal of Core Emotional Clearing. Bracken found his real self, which he had been searching for externally all his life, and felt his vast and boundless love.

CHAPTER 27

A FEW LAST WORDS

The work feels good afterwards, not during

Our emotional wounding consists of unfelt emotions related to pain and trauma, not joy. So we know in advance that feeling the emotions of our wounds will be uncomfortable. It is only after the process is complete that we will feel better. Much better. Our fear decreases as we do the work because we experience the benefits and amazing things begin to happen.

As we do more Core Emotional Clearing, we also come to realize that though these emotions "feel bad" there is nothing "wrong" with them. The pain is not "bad." It is just energy moving through our body. It is simply another of life's experiences. Over time we stop fearing our unfelt painful emotions and, in fact, embrace them as part of who we are right now.

Integration

After doing Core Emotional Clearing, we might feel tired, or even wiped out, if the process was particularly deep. This is because we are still processing the shifting of emotional energy in our body. The length of time it takes to integrate our unwinding of emotional energy depends upon how much energy we moved and our own individual makeup.

How long it takes to heal

There is no set time period for how long it takes to heal. There can be a gigantic shift from one healing experience, as with Suzanne, or there may be many healing experiences over several years. It all depends on the person, the circumstances and our ability to surrender.

We have to want to do the work

Core Emotional Clearing is an active process. It is not done to us. Nobody can wave a wand so that everything will suddenly be peachy. The essence of Core Emotional Clearing is feeling our emotions. Nobody can force us to feel. We have to want to do the work and take the steps to gain our freedom.

Similarly, the same holds true for our partner or anybody else in our life. No matter how great we might think Core Emotional Clearing would be for other people, it is no use trying to force the work onto them. They too have to want to do it. The first ingredient of anybody's Core Emotional Clearing is willingness.

As we have seen, our lack of willingness originates in the fears generated by our false identity. By contrast, our willingness stems from our innate desire to know our real self. We become tired of being separated from our love. We desire to open our heart again. We want the light of our love to move freely again.

We have an instinctive desire to connect to our light. The way to our light, however, is through the dark energy of our emotional wounding that physically blocks it. Our false identity can fool us into believing that in order to connect more to our light we need to focus on the light. Also, in our society we are often taught to focus on the light and ignore the dark. However, when we ignore the dark energy of our wounding we live a lie that has a very serious, and negative, impact on our life. Because of the very nature of emotional energy, the way to access our light is to voyage through our darkness. We then clear our darkness and, as a result, become more connected to our light.

Bonnie Serratore, mystic and shaman, is an expert at detecting the root cause of energy blocks within the physical, emotional, mental and spiritual bodies, as well as in releasing, removing, and clearing emotional energy, foreign energy and disincarnate beings from the physicality.

Bonnie is a teacher of healers and leads workshops and seminars at spiritual and wellness organizations. Her commitment and life purpose is to uplift consciousness, empower the individual, accelerate soul evolution and facilitate a freer expression of one's self. She is a resource for Young President Organization as an energy consultant, workshop facilitator and group dynamics guide.

Werner Disse was born in San Francisco and has lived in Switzerland, South Africa, France and Germany. He received a BA and MBA from Stanford University and a law degree from Oxford University, which he attended on a Rhodes Scholarship. Core Emotional Clearing, as described in The Way Back Home, is what he wishes he had learned in school.

CPSIA information can be obtained at www.ICGtesting.com
Printed in the USA
LVOW07s0735181014

409207LV00005B/48/P